Praise for *The Idol of Our Age*

"Daniel Mahoney is one of those true intellectuals whose wide reading feeds into and is fed by his experience of life. Few writers today are so aware of the pervasive influence of ideas, especially among those who have no ability to grasp them. In this study of the religion of humanity, Mahoney shows the great damage done by forgetting that man is made in God's image. His devastating criticisms are backed up with refined studies of thinkers who today are unjustly neglected, partly because they saw what is at stake in the religion of humanity. Those thinkers do not agree about the alternative to humanitarian ways of thinking, but they are united in their belief that being human consists in the search for something higher than the human. I recommend this book to all who share that belief, and who want to know exactly why it should be adhered to."

—Roger Scruton, writer and philosopher

"In times like these, when so much is deeply unsettled in both the Church and the world, there are few reliable guides to our predicament. But one has just appeared: Daniel Mahoney's brief but powerful book *The Idol of Our Age*."

—Robert Royal, *The Catholic Thing*

"To believers who have noticed a disconcerting distortion of Christianity's ideals of love and charity, Daniel Mahoney's *The Idol of Our Age: How the Religion of Humanity Subverts Christianity* may be a godsend."

—Chandler Lasch, *RealClearReligion*

"As an account of the ways in which the earthly and heavenly cities tend to get fused and confused these days, I recommend this book with enthusiasm."

—Travis D. Smith, *Convivium*

"Mahoney is no facile optimist or facile pessimist. He's a prophet calling us to listen with the heart, avoid the humanitarian siren song, and heed the civilizing memories of some fig⸻ ⸻ ⸻ little remembered.... Short and suggestive while also full-bodi⸻ ⸻ *Our Age* is a guidebook to the spiritual ⸻ s we are spiritual."

—⸻ *view*

"As ambitious as its subject might sound, the book delivers."
—Juliana Geran Pilon, *Law & Liberty*

"I found this to be an impressive approach to a very timely and essential issue....Daniel Mahoney is an unapologetic Christian thinker, and he presents a cogent case."
—Father Steven Kostoff, *Orthodox Christian Meditations*

"Mahoney's book is deep and well-researched. But it's highly readable. I'm finishing it slowly because each chapter sparks so much thought. And entices further reading."
—John Zmirak, *The Stream*

"As a firm Catholic realist, Mahoney must exercise his own courage, moderation, prudence, and justice in speaking truth to two of the regnant moral authorities of his own time....In so doing, and particularly in his chapter on the pope, he even illustrates what might be described as statesmanlike scholarship."
—Will Morrisey, *VoegelinView*

"Daniel Mahoney's new book, *The Idol of Our Age*, offers a sharp indictment of the humanitarianism that has become the implicit faith of our time....Mahoney offers a helpful corrective to the thought and feelings that have become instinctive in our politics and in Christian communities."
—Nathaniel Peters, *Public Discourse*

"But his is a message that our world urgently needs."
—Alexandra Hudson, *Catholic Herald*

"*The Idol of Our Age* seeks to reconnect rationality to a larger tradition of thought."
—Gerald J. Russello, *City Journal*

"Three themes emerge from Mahoney's treatment of the subject that identify the most salient characteristics of our 'shrug of the shoulders' moment: a rejection of the reality of sin and evil, an irrational trust in humanity, and a commensurate loss of faith in God."
—Casey Chalk, *The American Conservative*

The Idol of Our Age

The Idol of Our Age

*How the Religion of Humanity
Subverts Christianity*

Daniel J. Mahoney

BOOKS

New York • London

First American edition published in 2018 by Encounter Books,
an activity of Encounter for Culture and Education, Inc.,
a nonprofit, tax-exempt corporation.
Encounter Books website address: www.encounterbooks.com

Manufactured in the United States and printed on
acid-free paper. The paper used in this publication meets
the minimum requirements of ANSI/NISO Z39.48–1992
(R 1997) (*Permanence of Paper*).

First paperback edition published in 2020.
Paperback edition ISBN: 978-1-64177-092-7

THE LIBRARY OF CONGRESS HAS CATALOGUED
THE HARDCOVER EDITION AS FOLLOWS:

Names: Mahoney, Daniel J., 1960– author.
Title: The idol of our age : how the religion
of humanity subverts Christianity / by Daniel J. Mahoney.
Description: New York : Encounter Books, 2018. |
Includes bibliographical references and index.
Identifiers: LCCN 2018003458 (print) | LCCN 2018035438 (ebook) |
ISBN 9781641770170 (ebook) | ISBN 9781641770163 (hardcover : alk. paper)
Subjects: LCSH: Christianity—Essence, genius, nature. |
Humanitarianism—Religious aspects—Christianity. | Humanitarianism. |
Faith and reason. | Christianity and politics.
Classification: LCC BT60 (ebook) | LCC BT60 .M325 2018 (print) | DDC 230—dc23
LC record available at https://lccn.loc.gov/2018003458

Interior page design and composition: BooksByBruce.com

For Alain Besançon
Remarkable scholar, devoted friend,
and scourge of the totalitarian and humanitarian Lies

Contents

Preface to the Paperback Edition

As the author of *The Idol of Our Age*, I have been delighted that this profoundly countercultural reflection has received such a respectful, thoughtful, and, at times, enthusiastic reception since its original publication in December 2018. I have told numerous interviewers that the book seems to have struck a chord among serious Christians (Catholic, Protestant, and Orthodox alike), as well as with thoughtful non-believers who remain committed to the best of Western civilization. I believe that it has done so by giving a name to, and providing a serious analysis of, a multifaceted Western cultural pathology: the religion of humanity. This ersatz religion is a mix of doctrinaire egalitarianism, aggressive secularism, and fanatical humanitarianism that has become the substitute for transcendental religion, sober political thinking, and, in general, for realism and moderation in human affairs throughout the Western world.

Readers have welcomed the sustained analysis of the sources of this new religion, starting with August Comte's combination of scientific positivism, with its deep aversion to theology, metaphysics, and traditional morality, and a new morality where humanity itself would become "the Grand-Être," the new deity to be worshipped by man. Hence the religion of humanity. Like his fellow nineteenth-century sociological thinker, Karl Marx, Comte was an enemy of human liberty rightly understood and had contempt for the old religions and nations. He advocated a thoroughgoing deChristianization and depoliticization of the West, one where transcendent religion and political self-government would disappear. "Altruism," that is, humanitarian sentimentality, would replace Biblical love of God and man. The necessity for the defense of freedom and civilization—and, with them, war—would disappear. This prototype of a new religion was at once hubristic and utopian, and it was anti-human in its humanitarianism.

As I argued in the book, even Comte and Marx would be startled by the extent to which contemporary Christian self-understanding has come to confuse itself with humanitarianism in one form or another. Moral and personal self-limitation has given way to the pursuit of a liberationist and emancipatory cultural project, while contempt for the old Christian nations and support for a "world-governing authority" has replaced the search for the political common good by distinct political communities. Fanatical egalitarianism bids to replace a measured cultivation of our common humanity combined with respect for the authoritative institutions that are necessary elements of free political communities. In the process, love and charity have taken on a wholly "horizontal" dimension, increasingly estranged from the supernatural destiny of human beings. The old and enduring verities give way to the spirit of the age, to what an astute Catholic political philosopher has called the "authority of the present moment." In this new dispensation, the Good is historicized, nothing permanent is said to endure, and Christian political expectations become hopelessly utopian, fixated on an immanent transformation of human nature and the world. Progressive Christians are increasingly ignorant of the sempiternal drama of good and evil in the individual human soul. Mercy is always on their lips, but seldom, if ever, do we hear a call for repentance and *metanoia* of the soul.

When "the present moment" replaces what T. S. Eliot called "the Permanent Things," the soul is no longer called to be informed by the cardinal virtues of courage, temperance, justice, and prudence, or elevated by the theological ones of which St. Paul spoke: faith, hope, and love. In place of the virtues so central to human flourishing and salvation, one finds multiple examples of Christians inebriated by ideology. It was Max Scheler, the great German philosopher, however, who, during his long Catholic phase, reminded us that "Repentance, not Utopia, is the greatest revolutionary force in the world." On all these fronts, our progressives, liberationists, and humanitarians run the grave risk of substituting counterfeit goods for real ones. As Winston Churchill once said, "All wisdom is not new wisdom." We should be very hesitant, indeed, to dismiss the tried-and-true wisdom of the past, wisdom confirmed by revelation, right reason, and human experience.

In particular, the Christian world has largely lost an appreciation of a notion central to both classical philosophy and biblical religion: mediation. God chose his people Israel to be a light unto the nations. Jesus, the Incarnate Son of God, allows us to see the face of God, hitherto invisible. In general, as Pierre Manent has argued, we have no "immediate" access to the universal, except through the institutions in which we live. But Church elites and too many intellectuals have abandoned or repudiated the idea of mediation. In politics, the common good is no longer to be sought in self-governing nations (who, if faithful to the Christian inheritance, must repudiate undue hostility, not to mention homicidal aversion, to other self-governing peoples and nations). Contemporary papal thought does not even give a moment's attention to whether open borders and limitless migration would undermine what is left of the Christian character—or freedoms—of the Western world. Islam is declared a "religion of peace" against considerable evidence to the contrary. Concern for the distinctive character and existence of free peoples is ignored, or willfully dismissed as an anachronism. There, however, is nothing specifically Christian about these attitudes or the currently fashionable contempt for the nation. Cardinal Robert Sarah speaks the truth with rare courage and insight: a "globalized humanity, without borders," would be nothing less than "Hell" on earth.

Meanwhile, the pontificate of Pope Francis moves into an openly post-Catholic phase. His trusted interlocutor, the nonagenarian socialist and atheist journalist Eugenio Scalfari, reports that the Pope told him that he believes that, while on earth, Jesus was merely an outstanding man and not the Incarnate Lord. This is a sentiment worthy of Voltaire, Jefferson, or Tolstoy, not the Vicar of Christ. Nor was this the first such disconcerting report; earlier, Scalfari had said the Argentinian pope had told him that evil men's souls are annihilated and there is no Hell. An acolyte of the Pope, Father Arturo Sosa, S. J., the Venezuelan leftist who heads the Society of Jesus, brazenly declared the Devil is just a symbol and, earlier, that no one had a tape recorder when our Lord Jesus Christ set forth his demanding teachings on marriage and divorce. What a mockery these evasions and heterodox mutterings make of the integrity of the Catholic faith! And too many Catholics respond to such disturbing distortions of Christian teaching as if the pope is an oriental potentate who can change Catholic teaching and the natural moral law at will. St. John Henry Newman would shudder to hear "the voice of God" and the moral law glibly identified with historicized moral laxity and watered-down doctrine.

A misplaced ultramontanism leads many to remain silent as the subversion of Catholic teaching and classical wisdom proceeds apace. As for church leaders confronting these doctrinal and moral aberrations, too many bishops would prefer to talk about climate change, plastics, or the Amazonian rain forest, that is, about subjects about which they have no special expertise, to say the least. They risk becoming global activists at the service of a humanitarian NGO that no longer mediates the grace and goodness of God. This is a moral and spiritual abdication of the first order. Where, one must ask, is the courage of Thomas More, John Fisher, and the Catholic martyrs of the twentieth century who faced totalitarianism with great resolve?

Of course, there are those with opened eyes and clear voices. I have already mentioned the great Cardinal Sarah. Cardinal Gerhard Muller, the former head of the Congregation for the Defense of the Faith, told *The Catholic World Report* recently that there is "growing confusion in the Church" and he has done much to address it. A few others could be mentioned; alas, they are very much a minority among the episcopacy. Its loudest voices are ideologues for whom, as Cardinal Muller says, "global warming is more important than the awareness that God is the source and goal of man and of the whole creation." Our counterfeit Christians— humanitarians holding on to a small residue of the historic faith, appear to believe that "modern man can understand [Jesus] only as a moral preacher on environmental protection—not on sexual morality, of course."

Amid this immense moral and intellectual confusion and crisis, the Holy Father calls for a "Global Educational Alliance" to promote humanitarian values and activism that will culminate in a summit in Rome on May 14, 2020. Nothing is said of God or Christ, and this humanitarian agenda and alliance consists almost exclusively of left-wing ideological clichés. Since the writing and publication of my book, it has become apparent that the Holy Roman Pontiff no longer wishes to dissemble his radically humanitarian agenda. Nearly completely silent about the "crimes and sins" of sexual abuse that cry out for repentance (as well as the appropriate legal punishment), he has become a preacher of facile Third Worldism and ecological apocalypticism, all perfectly compatible with a humanitarian ethos essentially at odds with Christianity. He ignores the authoritative teaching of the Catholic catechism and of his two immediate predecessors, especially in the area of moral theology. If this moral and intellectual "paradigm shift" continues, if the Franciscan Revolution succeeds in permanently "changing the Church," the Catholic Church will, in important respects, cease to be the "barque of Peter" in the ample sense of the term. It will henceforth defer to the *zeitgeist*, come what may. The crisis, in my view, is just that grave.

We increasingly inhabit a world without heroes and saints, a world in which the capacity to admire what is truly admirable is deeply undermined. Humanitarian sloganeering is "cheap grace" for modern men and women. The arduous demands of the moral and intellectual virtues, of charity worth its salt, of true magnanimity and humility (which St. Thomas reminds us need not be in opposition) are relegated to a world modern man has definitively left behind. This must be resisted. It, in fact, is the true resistance in our time.

In conclusion, permit me to acknowledge two reviewers, Will Morrisey at *Voegelinview* and Steven H. Frankel in *Interpretation*, who perfectly understood that my critique of humanitarianism in *The Idol of Our Age* was at the service of melding Christian conscience, rooted in the natural moral law, with prudence, the preeminent moral and political virtue—"the god of this world below," as the great Edmund Burke famously put it. I am a self-conscious partisan of both Christian faith and political reason of a broadly classical sort. Without a renewal of a reason open to faith, of a "richer, higher form of reason" that speaks to the needs of the soul and those of civilized freedom and order, neither believers nor non-believers can make their way in the world. As Prof. Frankel put it, authentic reason "does not peremptorily reject the possibility of a moral order or access to the account of the whole." Such a capacious reason can give us access once again to all the tension-ridden resources of Jerusalem, Athens, and Rome. It can protect our minds and souls from the temptation to rest content with a religion of humanity that combines the worst of progressivism and humanitarianism, forgetting both the "listening heart" (I Kings 3:9) that allows us to discern good and evil and the intellectual virtues that allow us to discern the vital distinction between truth and falsehood. When the Pontifical John Paul II Institute is subject of a Stalinist purge to get rid of all theologians who, faithful to magisterial Catholic teaching, believe that there are human acts and choices that are intrinsically evil, the Church risks leaving behind the framework of good and evil, truth and falsehood, in the name of an authority devoid of all content: the spirit of the times and the authority of "the present moment." What a poor, emasculated substitute for the light of enduring truth! And what an abandonment of the Gospel and the natural law!

Let us in contrast heed the wisdom of Cardinal Robert Sarah, so richly articulated in the recently published *The Day Is Now Far Spent.* With great insight, wisdom, and passion, the great African cardinal laments the "golden calf" of humanitarianism that makes us indifferent to true religion and true virtue, and is undermining the very soul of civilization. Sarah writes:

> The dream of the Western globalized elite is precisely to establish a new world religion. For this little group, the ancient religions, and in particular the Catholic Church, must be transformed or die. They must abandon their doctrine and moral teaching. It is supposedly necessary to arrive at a worldwide, global religion, a religion without God, without doctrine, and without moral teaching.

This is the religion of a post-political, post-Christian world, where facile relativism quickly gives rise to toxic and coercive moralism. This witch's brew of relativism and moralism must not be allowed to capture the hearts and souls of the Churches. This is not a time for passivity! It is a time when reason open to faith, and religion respectful of reason, must unite to defend a freedom worthy of man. When we dogmatically separate reason and religion, facts and values, we open the doors to an ideological representation of reality that is closed to both and to their common humanizing affirmation of sacred limits and restraints. My hope is that *The Idol of Our Age* has contributed in its small way to the reinvigoration of true reason and true religion, and thus to a rejection of the ideological substitutes for them. Perhaps as never before, we are today obliged to resist the ideological assault on the truth and the sovereignty of God and his moral law. This is true even, or especially, if it is put forth in the name of "Humanity."

Daniel J. Mahoney
Worcester, Massachusetts
October 15, 2019

Foreword

By Pierre Manent

With this book, Daniel J. Mahoney has written a timely, lucid, and convincing analysis, and a damning indictment, of the most widespread and disabling moral distemper of our time. Let me try to cut through its richness and complexity and bring out the nerve of the argument.

Under the blanket term "humanitarianism," Professor Mahoney encapsulates a pervasive and authoritative opinion that is the single most powerful factor in the shaping of our public and private thoughts, feelings, and actions. It is an opinion that commands and forbids, inspires and intimidates: it is a *ruling* opinion. I would summarize it in the following way: Peace and unity belong to the natural condition of mankind; conversely, its fragmentation into separate political bodies solicitous of their independence is the toxic fountainhead of everything that is wrong in human circumstances. Thus the right thing to do, the worthy enterprise, is to bring about the pacification and unification of humanity through the erasing or weakening of borders, the acceleration of the circulation of goods, services, information, and human beings, the fostering of an ever stronger and wider fellow-feeling among countries and peoples. Accordingly, looking at human things from the perspective of one's own community—its common good and the peculiar content and quality of its education and way of life—is intrinsically wrong because it amounts to turning one's back on the rest of mankind. Looking at human things in terms of the imminent or growing unification of mankind, of what is common to all human beings—thus looking at human things without the least preference (and even with a tad of healthy dislike) for what is ours—is intrinsically right and "progressive." Such is the ruling opinion of our time that Professor Mahoney submits to a searching examination.

Under the guise of a seductive impartiality or universality, this "humanitarianism" involves a general scrambling of the reference points from which human beings, as moral agents and free citizens, take their bearings. If we find less and less to love and admire, even to understand, in the human associations to which we belong and from which we draw the greatest part of our moral and intellectual resources, and instead entertain a principled preference for what is foreign, far off, in general "other"—that is, what is beyond the range of our practical knowledge and real experience—then what Professor Mahoney calls our "moral cognition" is impaired, indeed gravely warped. Pretending to be the happy denizens of a world composed of an indefinite variety of cultures, all equally worthy of the same respect, we live in a make-believe moral world in which ideology reigns supreme, since there is no real and sincere experience behind this declamatory respect. We are no longer citizens, members of the citizen-body, no longer moral agents partaking in a concrete tradition of moral experience and judgment, but rather "new men" committed to an inordinate and ultimately spurious experiment, that is, the producing of a "new humanity," a fake humanity cut off from its real resources, whether these belong to civic, moral, or religious life.

This perspective on human things—this "brave new world"—is not the result of a recent development, even though it has lately become especially overweening or intolerant. As Professor Mahoney luminously explains in the chapter devoted to Auguste Comte's "religion of humanity," this mental formation is coextensive with the specifically modern, or democratic, transformation of our social condition. With American independence and the French Revolution, Western people discovered that they could organize themselves without reference to a divine Law but rather according to human rights; once humankind has become the farthest and most authoritative horizon of human action, the idea of Humanity necessarily becomes the highest and most authoritative idea. Once the Christian God is no longer the keystone of the sacredness of the common, mankind itself is fated to become God—not in a metaphorical or loose sense, but in a politically relevant one: humankind is the only great thing that citizens can spontaneously and sincerely consider greater than themselves, the true Grand-Être. Thus Professor Mahoney's reconstitution of Auguste Comte's *religion de l'humanité* is not just some interesting inquiry belonging to the history of ideas; it is part and parcel of an urgent question addressed to every citizen and thinking being, at least in the Western world, since it is a matter of disentangling the Christian God from the humanitarian Grand-Être, or the other way around.

As everybody knows, there is a solid wall of separation between Church and State in our democratic regimes, and we are grateful for that. At the same time, this institutional arrangement does not solve all problems pertaining to our double nature as Christian citizens, if we happen to be Christian. Our amphibious character is made more uncomfortable with every step in the progress of the religion of humanity that suspends a haze of suspicion or illegitimacy above both our civilian and Christian lives. Instead of being separate, politics and religion risk becoming confused under the humanitarian dispensation, since the religion of humanity seems to make the State and the Church one.

As citizens, we need to be able to exercise our rights and fulfill our duties in a political association, the legitimacy of which is not subject to any disqualification in the name of "humanity," as when the lawful government of a nation is said to have no right to determine what persons it will accept within its borders, since migrants are only exercising their human rights. According to this view, human rights trump any and all arguments of political justice or prudence. As for those citizens who are Christian, they are forced to seriously ponder the authentic meaning and physiognomy of their religion, especially since they are constantly told that the effective truth of their religion lies with the humanitarian impulse and the religion of humanity. Professor Mahoney's book aims to dispel the confusion brought about by this meretricious religiosity and save the civic and Christian experiences from their humanitarian parody.

The question of the true meaning of Christianity is all the more perplexing and vexed because the public and private pronouncements of the current pope have incessantly contributed to the blurring of the wisest and most necessary distinctions. Professor Mahoney is admirably informed and equitable in his analysis and evaluation of Pope Francis's considered thinking.

His purpose is to contribute to an understanding of the articulation between the perspective of the citizen and the perspective of the Christian—an articulation that is distorted, indeed smashed, when we conflate the citizen and the Christian into a "citizen of the world" who sees no difference between nations or religions and sees his neighbor everywhere except among his fellow citizens. Through a close and acute reading of writings of the Russian philosopher Vladimir Soloviev, he elucidates how the temptation to conflate the two perspectives can arise and how it can be resisted, as it should be. To clarify in a very concrete way what it means to be a serious Christian acting as a good citizen in a given set of circumstances, Professor Mahoney has recourse to the historical and literary inquiry conducted by Aleksandr Solzhenitsyn in the context of Russian history, especially the March 17 Revolution. What the great Russian writer, of whom Mr. Mahoney is today the most competent and judicious interpreter, makes clear is that Christian virtues cannot consist in sapping or gelding civic virtues. While Christians necessarily aim for farther or higher objectives, their virtues as citizens fully belong to the cardinal virtues they share with their agnostic or atheist fellow citizens. They ought to be courageous, moderate, just, and prudent—a tall order that they should not elude or shirk in the name of an indiscriminate "love" or "openness."

The heart of the challenge lies in what Professor Mahoney, following Alain Besançon, calls the "falsification of the good." What makes humanitarianism or the religion of humanity so alluring is that it gives its adepts the certainty of doing good as well as the feeling of being good, all the more so because in the world of fellow-feeling, most of the doing lies in the feeling. It is an offer that is difficult to resist! What is decisive is the purported evidence and easiness of the good, which simply consists in acknowledging and appreciating the similitude of the "other." The least objection or reticence elicits burning indignation: How can you not see that the good is good? When "being good" seems to be synonymous with being a human being and acknowledging that "the other" is a human being too, how can you bring distinctions and arguments into the debate? How can you even *reason*? How can you not see that a bridge is good and a wall is bad?

With a deft and sure hand, Daniel Mahoney limns the outlines, the rhythm, of a serious moral deliberation. Instead of trusting the often superficial or deceitful evidence of the good, be alert to the ineradicable sway of evil! Discriminating between good and evil, right and wrong, is *the* theme of practical life. Making oneself capable of this discrimination necessitates a long and exacting education of this impartial, but too often lazy or too easily bribed, judge that the Western tradition calls conscience. We need a well-educated and well-trained conscience to meet the challenges of private and political life. An easygoing fellow-feeling will not do. It will only fall prey to the falsification of the good.

The denizens of the Western world live under the pressure of an unholy proposition pushed by the State and the ruling elites, including many senior figures of the churches, which I would summarize in the following way: obedience to law and the call of duty is not an essential part of the effort toward a full and good life; evil, however deplorable, is not an implacable enemy requiring our constant vigilance and resistance, it is an inconvenience that will progressively peter out as we jettison old stereotypes and new suspicions and acknowledge with open hearts, and without delay, the goodness of others. An open heart summarizes the only real meaning of goodness or virtue, since the only root of evil is our own reluctance to open our hearts to the goodness of others. Professor Mahoney makes a very cogent argument that this way of thinking entails the inglorious death of civic virtue, as well as of serious attention to the Christian proposition. With rigorous historical and philosophical arguments, he reconstitutes the pedigree of this "new morality" and argues convincingly for a recovery of the right understanding of civic life—that is, devoted to the common good—and Christian life—that is, devoted to the highest, more than human good. His is a generous and virile argument for the arduousness of what is just and noble, as well as for the justice and nobility of what is arduous.

The Secular Religion of Our Age

The book you are about to read is a learned essay at the intersection of politics, philosophy, and theology. It is a diagnosis and critique of the secular religion of our age: humanitarianism, or what I also call "the religion of humanity." Writing in 1944, the Hungarian moral and political philosopher Aurel Kolnai had already noted the tendency of people in a democratic age to take their bearings from "man as such," who, in this view, is seen as the "measure of everything." That which is above man is forgotten or taken for granted, if not openly repudiated. This humanitarian impulse had already begun to corrupt Christianity itself, reducing it to an inordinate concern for "social welfare," for the alleviation of poverty and suffering in all its forms. In progressive secular and religious circles, humanitarianism was seen as the effectual truth of Christianity, which no longer needed transcendental reference points. Kolnai, our deepest philosophical guide to the difference between the authentically religious attitude and the new humanitarian ethos, will make more than one appearance in this book. With rare penetration, he saw the inability of humanitarianism to come to terms with the drama of good and evil in the human soul. "Society" (whatever that is) would be increasingly blamed for evil and criminality, and legitimate punishment would be dismissed as distasteful, if not barbaric. Yet humanitarians enthusiastically welcome abortion and euthanasia and make them mandatory parts of a regime of human rights. We are living in a world turned upside down, a world marked by moral inversion.

One Kolnai-influenced scholar, Graham McAleer, has pointed out that three states—California, New Jersey, and Washington—allow children to sue doctors for failing to abort them. In this perverse understanding, non-being is preferable to the pain and suffering that accompany a disability. Such are the consequences of a humanitarian ethics based on a hedonistic and relativistic calculus that recognizes neither intrinsic good (that is, the sanctity of life) or intrinsic evil (such as the killing of innocents). Humanitarianism is the direct result of what McAleer calls "a bold assertion of human sovereignty that necessarily abolishes the sovereignty of the moral object, and therewith God's sovereignty." It is the self-conscious negation of a natural order of things, an objective hierarchy of moral goods, accessible to human beings through natural reason, conscience, and common sense. To live in such a world is to lose one's moral bearings. A cursory reflection shows that humanitarianism subverts Christianity and the moral law and leaves nothing but confusion in their place.

As a result, relativism coexists with limitless moralism. This is the most striking feature of the modern "moral" order. Left-wing humanitarians and "progressive" churchmen spout on about "social justice" as if opponents of doctrinaire egalitarianism hate the poor or support social injustice. But they never really tell us what "social justice" is or what the adjective adds to the noun. The taking of an unborn life is merely a "choice," which is, one assumes, completely beyond good and evil. And who can be against free choice? To argue that marriage has some link to the complementarity of men and women and to natural procreation (and is also at the service of the education of new citizens) is somehow to subvert a love which need not respect natural distinctions. And who can be against love? Free choice, autonomous choice, trumps any respect for the directedness of human freedom toward natural ends or purposes. A kind of juvenile existentialism, marked more by farce than angst, has become the default position of our age.

One of the great contributions of the Christian proposition to a conception of liberty and human dignity worthy of man has been its "revolutionary" message that "all men are brothers and sisters and have one and the same Father. We are equal in dignity, for we are all created in the image of God." But as Cardinal Robert Sarah, the author of these lines, points out in his magisterial book *God or Nothing*, the fatherhood of God and the brotherhood of man in no way entail or demand "fanatical egalitarianism." Sarah grew up in Guinea under the totalitarian rule of Sékou Touré. He saw how the promise of absolute equality destroyed liberty and human dignity and led to true misery and tens of thousands of deaths. Fanatical egalitarianism is an invitation to unabashed tyranny. Sarah draws the appropriate conclusions: The divine and natural orders require difference and complementarity and not a homogenizing egalitarianism. Radical egalitarianism wars with the highest in human beings and thus mutilates man. Sarah bravely notes that "today gender theory seems to be toying with the same illusory battle for equality." Whether in the form of Marxist-Leninism or fanatical efforts to efface natural sexual differences, doctrinaire egalitarianism reveals the destructive face of utopia cut off from God and a natural order of things. It is anti-human in decisive respects.

This book does not hesitate to deal with the perplexity that is Pope Francis. In doing so, I write as a Catholic layman and as a political philosopher respectful of the office of the pope. For the first time in the history of the Church, we have a pope who is half-humanitarian and thoroughly blind to the multiple ways in which humanitarian secular religion subverts authentic Christianity. With winks and nods, he challenges the age-old Catholic teaching that there are intrinsic evils that cannot be countenanced by a faithful Christian or any person of good will. In a thousand ways, he sows confusion in the Church and the world. His views on politics are summary, to say the least, and partake of the inordinate egalitarianism against which Cardinal Sarah properly warns. Pope Francis has displayed indulgence toward left-wing tyrannies that are viciously anti-Catholic to boot. His views on Islam are equally summary and partake of an unthinking political correctness (the Koran, he insists against all evidence, always demands nonviolence). He has spoken respectfully about Communism, the murderous scourge of the twentieth century. All of this is perplexing for the faithful Christian, to say the least.

More recently, he has openly flirted with pacifism. Christianity is a morally demanding religion that requires imperfect human beings to forgive their enemies. It is incompatible with terrorism, wars of aggression, and cruelty of any sort. But the order of charity demands that legitimately constituted authorities protect those under their care from violence, tyranny, and aggression. As Roger Scruton has put it, "the right of defense stems from your obligations to others." The Sermon on the Mount is not a call for societal suicide or even a guide to public policy. As scholars have noted, Christ's "effusive" praise for the Roman centurion on the road to Capernaum (Matthew 8:5–13) is hardly compatible with pacifism. Yet in a recent book of interviews with a French social scientist, Pope Francis declares that "no war is just" and that one "always wins with peace." He has obviously not considered "the peace of the grave" and the "soulless despotism" that so preoccupied Immanuel Kant. By seemingly siding with peace at any price, he prevents statesmen, Christian statesmen, from carrying out their responsibilities to justice and the common good. In the same book of interviews, Francis forthrightly blames modern war on money, a crude and reductionist account that ignores the manifestly political, even spiritual, reasons for human conflict. And he seems to think terrorists are motivated by economic deprivation rather than blind hatred or fanatical religious passion. The pope's thinking on these matters is strangely economistic, even para-Marxist, and shows no engagement with the rich and varied motives—rooted in pleasure, virtue, the noble, the just, anger at injustice, the ambition to rule or even change the world—that animate the souls of men. One expects more expertise in the soul from the Holy Roman Pontiff, and not the crude and reductive economism he regularly displays.

I will not give a point-by-point summary of what is to follow. I will leave the adventure of discovery to the reader. Suffice it to say, I take my bearings from a series of profound thinkers who have gotten to the heart of this strange new beast called humanitarianism. Pope Benedict XVI has taught us all that Christianity is in no way reducible to "a humanitarian moral message." Raymond Aron and Eric Voegelin have provided essential insights for understanding Auguste Comte's self-conscious "religion of humanity." Comte remains one of the secret rulers of our world, pointing the way to human self-deification and an evisceration of authentic political life. Pierre Manent has taught me how the de-Christianization of the modern world goes hand in hand with its depoliticization. He is that rare Christian who knows how to think politically.

The book also serves to introduce to readers three "prophets" who appreciated the full import of both the "totalitarian" and "humanitarian" lies long before their contemporaries: Orestes Brownson (1803–1876), Vladimir Soloviev (1853–1900), and Aurel Kolnai (1900–1973). The American Brownson was an adherent of the "religion of humanity" before becoming a Catholic and a constitutional republican; his odyssey is an instructive journey to truth and self-understanding. He saw it all coming *avant la lettre*. Like Soloviev, Aleksandr Solzhenitsyn shows thoughtful readers of his *Red Wheel* that evil must be resisted by force and that pacifism is a grave and terrible temptation for the Christian and the citizen alike. Yet he never lost his humanity or sense of moderation. I should add that all the thinkers on whom I have drawn are men of peace, which is precisely why they reject ideological pacifism and the confusion of Christianity with an unthinking sentimentality.

Two brief final chapters address, respectively, the influential German social theorist Jürgen Habermas's plea for a post-national world (an essential element of humanitarian ideology) and how conscience, properly understood, is our portal for recovering "the sovereignty of the object," a world where the distinctions between the true and the false, and good and evil, are not merely arbitrary. Reason, as well as revealed faith, gives us access to an order of things. We are not adrift in the world, forced to choose between moral anarchy and nihilistic despair.

The Introduction and Chapters One, Two, Three, and Eight appear in this book for the first time. I thank *First Things*, *Logos*, and *The Hungarian Review* for permission to republish material in other chapters, albeit in significantly revised form.

Many thanks to Pierre Manent, Giulio de Ligio, and Philippe Bénéton for being faithful interlocutors on all matters related to philosophy, religion, and politics. They are dear and trusted friends and make my sojourns in Paris wonderfully worthwhile. I dedicate this book to another friend, the great French philosophical historian, Russianist, and amateur theologian Alain Besançon. He introduced me to the writing of the great Soloviev, with his incomparable short story of the "humanitarian" Antichrist, and helped me better appreciate that authentic Christianity has nothing to do with sentimentality, humanitarianism, pacifism, or hatred of the real. He is one of the great scholars and teachers of the age.

Finally, many thanks to Roger Kimball at Encounter for seeing the promise in this book and to Vanessa Silverio and Katherine Wong for their expert work along the way.

As befitting a book of this sort, each chapter concludes with a brief bibliographical section ("Sources and Suggested Readings") rather than a scientific, scholarly apparatus.

• SOURCES AND SUGGESTED READINGS •

For more on Kolnai, see Chapter Four of this book and his 1944 article "The Humanitarian versus the Religious Attitude," which appears as an Appendix to the book.

I am indebted to G. J. McAleer's *To Kill Another: Homicide and Natural Law* (New Brunswick, NJ: Transaction Publishers, 2012).

For a thoughtful reflection on the confusions that accompany talk about "social justice," see Carrie Gress, "What Exactly Is Social Justice?" in the *National Catholic Register*, March 3, 2016. Gress points out that unilateral appeals to social justice, choice, and love are means of closing off conversation and deliberation.

For a lucid and persuasive critique of fanatical egalitarianism, see Robert Cardinal Sarah, *God or Nothing: A Conversation on Faith with Nicolas Diat* (San Francisco: Ignatius Press, 2015), p. 190.

For Pope Francis on matters of war and peace, see Pape François, *Recontres avec Dominique Wolton: Politique et Société* (Paris: Éditions de L'Observatoire, 2017), pp. 57–58, 94.

CHAPTER ONE

The Humanitarian Subversion of Christianity and Authentic Political Life

The great danger of contemporary humanitarianism is of habituating peoples to despise political reflection, even politics itself and its concrete conditions of existence, as if the affirmation of humanity was sufficient in itself.

Each epoch knows some temptations. The revolutionary temptation persisted for a long time in the West. Today, we experience the humanitarian temptation, which appears more sympathetic. But, in a certain manner, these two temptations are in continuity, and belong to the very same project: to abolish the political existence of men which separates human beings into nations and classes.

— PIERRE MANENT (2000)

The distinguished French Catholic political thinker Pierre Manent perfectly describes the humanitarian temptation that afflicts the Western world today. Even as we insist that human beings live in closed cultures, utterly sufficient unto themselves, our elites blindly announce the unification of a "humanity" which is escaping national loyalties and national identification. Unbeknownst to ourselves, we are adherents of nineteenth-century French philosopher and sociologist Auguste Comte's "religion of humanity." Comte was the "prophet" of the movement of humankind from a theological and military order to a scientific and industrial one, and of the dawn of a great "Occidental Republic" that would culminate in the comprehensive unity of the human race. He was the theorist of "democratic pantheism" par excellence since, in the future that he imagined and announced, there would be no more separation between either God and man or peoples and nations. Manent, following his teacher Raymond Aron, calls Comte "the sociologist of human and social unity." In this understanding, Humanity becomes its own paramount theme. The movement toward a unified humanity is "irresistible," but it must be "institutionalized and organized" through "the organization and institution of the religion of humanity." As Manent shows, Comte makes explicit the implicit faith of the late modern world.

Like Comte, Manent suggests, our intellectual elites "can only see human unity." The philosophical idea of humanity, which first came to light in the eighteenth century in French and German enlightenment thought, is now accompanied by what can only be described as "religious enthusiasm." What Montesquieu, Voltaire, and Kant announced as a humanizing "Idea" to soften and regulate the mores of modern peoples, we treat as a "self-evident truth." All who question it are met with "sacred indignation." Nations were seemingly discredited by the two world wars of the twentieth century, and, as a result, Europe, Comte's avant-garde of humanity, sees unity where it only incompletely exists. Human beings still live in political communities, plural nations, and regimes, which are the only homes we have for common action, for true political life. These communities "mediate" and "concretize" our sense of the universal but are met by our contemporaries with what Manent calls "vigilant hostility." We increasingly despise mediation and the political expression of our humanity. In truth, human beings experience common humanity only in the meeting of diverse human and spiritual affirmations and propositions that arise from the concrete human communities in which we live. We see and feel these communities every day. But our intellectuals and opinion-makers are prisoners of the "invisible" unity of the human race that only true believers can see. The humanitarian temptation takes the form of an intolerant and indignant "religion of humanity," which excoriates all those who do "not see humanity as an immediate reality," as a self-evident truth. In multiple ways, Auguste Comte remains the secret ruler of souls.

FROM POSITIVISM TO THE RELIGION OF HUMANITY

Auguste Comte was a theoretician of positivism before becoming the founder of the "religion of humanity." His atheism is more thoroughgoing than what usually goes by the name. He faulted most *soi-disant* atheists for still trying to answer metaphysical questions. "The true positive spirit" was aggressively anti-theological and anti-metaphysical. It regarded questions about the "why" of existence as utterly futile. True science was concerned with "the study of the invariable laws of phenomena," not with causes, whether "proximate or primary." It had no interest in explaining the formation of the universe or the origin of animal and human life. These were "metaphysical" concerns that would be left behind by the positivist spirit. The eminent twentieth-century political philosopher Eric Voegelin has noted the incipient totalitarianism lurking behind Comte's rendering of the great human questions as futile and useless. In the spirit of ideology, Comte simply announces that these questions can no longer be asked in the great Occidental Republic of which he is the prophet and forerunner. He imposes on reason a crippling self-limitation that prevents it from engaging in properly philosophical reflection. In this way, too, Comte remains a ruler of souls and is one of the sources of the flaccid positivism that dismisses out of hand those questions about truth and meaning that are at the core of our dignity as thinking animals.

In his chapter on the "Religion of Humanity" at the end of part I of his *System of Positive Polity*, Comte announces the superiority of the morality of positive science to the morality of revealed religion, since it has substituted "the love of Humanity for the love of God." Adverse to all forms of theology and metaphysics, and excluding "all personal considerations," the new morality puts "Social Feeling" above self-love. "Humanity," understood as the very best in human beings, becomes the Grand-Être to be worshipped by limited and fallible men. Comte has forgotten that what is highest in man finds its ultimate source in what is higher than man. Without deference to the Beings, Forms, and Limits that inform and elevate the human will, man risks becoming a monster to himself, enslaved by his own self-deification. Comte admirably recognized that people should defer to what is best, most meritorious, in human beings. But as Aurel Kolnai has well noted, nobility also entails "the subordination of everything human to what is above man." Men are not gods, and that affirmation is the beginning of all wisdom, secular and religious. Voegelin strikingly captures what is so disturbing in Comte's innovation: his is an "inter-mundane eschatology...a divination of word-immanent entities" that is the enemy of all transcendent reality. Nothing humane or truly spiritual can arise from such an "apocalypse of man." It is built on the most demonic of foundations—what Voegelin so suggestively calls in *Science, Politics, and Gnosticism* "the murder of God."

PSEUDO-CHRISTIAN ASSONANCES

Readers of Comte cannot help but be struck by what Voegelin calls the "Christian assonances" in his writings, the repeated appeals to "charity," "love," "spirituality," and "faith." But Voegelin rightly adds that we should not be deceived by this appeal to "religious" categories. The famous motto of the Comtean movement appeals to "Love," its "principle," to "Order," its "basis," and to "Progress," its "end." Comte aimed to bring Feeling, Reason, and Activity together in a perfect synthesis, one that would wholly supersede the old religion and any conception of God. Like all partisans of the end of History, he aimed for a "perfect harmony" where evil and sin would have no place. He would reconcile the aspirations of the French Revolution with the requirements of order, thus establishing a "restoration" on revolutionary foundations. Comte found spirituality in the harmonizing work of women, represented by that great love of his life, Clotilde de Vaux (1845 was the transformative year of their encounter), who taught him the existential primacy of the affective over the rational part of the soul. But love, for which he invented the term "altruism," was completely divorced from the *amor Dei*. As Voegelin pointed out, the soul was no longer directed to any transcendental reality. As Voegelin also astutely observed, Comte cannot fathom the existence of "evil spirits." He is blind to the depths of the soul. His account of a completely mundane "spiritual order" is thus deformed by a naïve faith that believes history will simply leave evil behind in the new, positive age. Comte's is the most superficial of anthropologies, since it is ignorant of the drama of good and evil in the human soul.

As Voegelin also observes, Comte spiritualizes utilitarianism in ways that are manifestly dangerous and illiberal. He speaks "with the authority of spirit," even though he has no place for the human soul or an order of things of which it is a part. His spiritual order embodies an "order of moral worth," a meritocracy within a technocratic industrial order. Woman, the proletariat, and the priests of the religion of humanity will temper and transfigure the hierarchies that constitute industrial society. All of this sounds harmless enough. But Comte was no mere technocrat or benign reformer. He proclaimed himself the "high priest" of Humanity, the exalted servant of the Grand-Être, and announced with great fanfare that the "*siècle exceptionel*," the new Occidental Republic dedicated to the religion of humanity, would be inaugurated in 1855. He drew up *The Catechism of Positive Religion* in the early 1850s and even concocted a *Calendrier* that would, as Voegelin puts it, pay tribute to the "great men who belong to the *Préparation Humaine* that leads up to the positive age." The religious founders, from Zoroaster and St. Paul to Mohammed, were given their places—save one, Jesus Christ. He who is truly God and truly Man, the God-man whose very existence refutes the illusions of pantheism and its perverse spiritualization of the immanent, shall not be mentioned or honored in the new, final age inaugurated by Comte. Comte takes the place of Christ, just as "the love of Humanity," the jealous Grand-Être, takes the place of "love of God." In this sense, Comte has divinized his own existence, making himself the herald of a new Humanity worshipping itself. Comte's existence, and Comte's alone, truly has universal significance as the harbinger of human self-deification.

A THIS-WORLDLY ESCHATOLOGY

Today, many join John Stuart Mill and Émile Littré in praising Comte's positivism, his dogmatic and unreasonable hostility to metaphysical speculation and inquiry, while decrying his decision to transform positivism into a religion. But at least Comte saw the need to buttress human unity with an enhanced emphasis on "social feeling," "altruism," and a "spiritual order" that transcended the requirements of technique. The problem is the resort to what Voegelin calls "an inter-mundane eschatology" that is inseparable from a philosophy of history that confuses prophetism for reality. And yet, without the fanfare or the accompanying catechism and calendar, many of our contemporaries remain wedded to a religious emphasis on human unity that thoughtlessly and resolutely leaves the old nations and the old religion behind. As Manent suggests, we smile at Comte, the High Priest of Humanity, even as we adhere to many of his secular "religious" presuppositions.

ADIEU TO POLITICS

If Voegelin is the most helpful guide to understanding the not always obvious eschatological dimensions of Comte's project, the great French political thinker Raymond Aron provides crucial guidance for understanding Comte's desire to abolish the political realm of human existence in its entirety. As Aron points out, Comte assumed that the positivist era, the age of science, industrial society, and a religion of human unity, would leave war behind once and for all. Europeans were the avant-garde of humanity, paving the way for the abolition of war and the full reconciliation of the human race. As Aron comments in *Main Currents of Sociological Thought*, history failed Auguste Comte in the years leading up to 1945.

But with the end of the Cold War, Europeans have proceeded as if they are indeed the harbingers of a post-political humanity that will leave borders and sovereignty behind. As Manent has argued in *Seeing Things Politically*, they can adhere to this quasi-Comtean religion of humanity largely because they continue to rely on the United States for their military protection. In the 1970s, in Aron's masterwork on Clausewitz, Aron himself called the "farewell to arms" "the great illusion" captivating the European mind and soul. He was convinced that Comte, like Marx, had woefully underestimated the political, imperial, and tragic dimensions of human history. "History as usual" would persist even in the age of science and technique, since human beings cannot escape being political animals. To believe otherwise was to give in to a hope supported only by faith. Comte may not have been wrong that Napoléon misjudged his age by hurling France into the conquest of Europe and by restoring a military regime in place of representative institutions. But the same Comte hated "representative and liberal institutions" and applauded Louis Napoléon's coup d'état in December 1851. Comte denounced British-style parliamentary institutions as the "metaphysical" instruments of windbags and had next to no concern for political liberty. He even wrote the Russian tsar a letter in the introduction to volume II of his *System of Positive Polity* offering to instruct him in the lessons of positive philosophy. Comte's concern for the "fundamental reorganization of European society" and the establishment of a unified human race was unsullied by any concern for political liberty or self-government.

Do contemporary adherents of the religion of humanity show much more respect for the self-government of nations and peoples? They, too, seem to treat political liberty as a metaphysical concern belonging to another moment in human history. In this connection, everyone observes the "democratic deficit" in the European project, but nothing is done about it. Elites affirm the "irresistible" character of "globalization" and the necessary erosion of civic life at the national level (is there a dirtier word today than "nationalism," which is almost always arbitrarily confused with humane national loyalty?). Like Comte's original positivism and its accompanying religion of humanity, contemporary partisans of human unity are all too happy to say goodbye to both politics and the Christian religion. Depoliticization and de-Christianization are two great preconditions of the movement toward a unified humanity, now freed from all need for political or religious mediation and concretization. Comte thus hovers in the background not as a prophet of a new age, of a new historical dispensation, but as the half-deluded theorist of a secular religion that remains the temptation of our age. The humanitarian lie is in important respects less horrifying than the totalitarian one, but it is rooted in the same contempt for the political nature of man and the same ignorance of the human soul. The illusions of humanitarianism remind us of the protean character of the ideological lie under conditions of modernity. At its center is a willful denial of the political and spiritual nature of man in any substantial sense of the terms.

CHRISTIANITY AND THE RELIGION OF HUMANITY

Humanitarianism, the softer, regnant version of the religion of humanity, is thus wholly at odds with the Christian proposition and the risks subverting it in the name of an inter-mundane eschatology. Woefully ignorant of sin and of the tragic dimensions of the human condition, it reduces religion to a project of this-worldly amelioration. Free-floating compassion substitutes for charity, and a humanity conscious of its unity (and utter self-sufficiency) puts itself in the place of the visible and invisible Church. Christians ought to be the most sensitive to what is at stake in this new and aggressive secular religion, but today they increasingly redefine the contents of the faith in broadly humanitarian terms. Christianity is shorn of any recognizable transcendental dimension and becomes an instrument for promoting egalitarian social justice, usually in the name of an ideological conception of the poor (clearly, Pope Francis increasingly fits into this category). One cannot help but ask if Christianity is inherently vulnerable to humanitarian appropriation, as Nietzsche suggested with hostile intent. Pierre Manent, with no hostile intent, has argued that the religion of humanity would never "have attained its empire over our souls if it did not appear as the extension and the consequence, perhaps the effectual truth, of Christianity, of the religion of the neighbor." Manent suggests that "the feeling of the same," the vague but powerful sentiment of a common humanity on the way to full realization in a unified human race, appears to many in the modern democratic world as "the truly human form, the final form of Christian charity."

But this reduction of charity, the greatest theological virtue, to compassion and fellow-feeling ignores the fact that genuine love of one's neighbor is only possible because one discerns in him or her "the image of God." Every unique and irreplaceable person reflects in some way the goodness and grandeur of God, and not his or her own self-sufficiency. Manent suggests that authentic love frees us from the double slavery to the self and the other because it elevates the soul to a higher spiritual plane, one marked by the ineffable grace and goodness of God. The Good Samaritan does not love the wounded man on the side of the road because he somehow espouses the "democratic religion of the same." He is not a humanitarian, but one who is properly sensitive to the image of God in each and every human being, however marked we all are by sin. The modern world has trouble understanding St. Mother Teresa of Calcutta because it can only interpret her good works within the closed horizons of humanitarianism. Mother Teresa, however, told Malcolm Muggeridge in the late 1960s that her love for the poorest of the poor was motivated by her desire to do "something beautiful for God." The paradox of Christian charity is that by escaping from the closed circle of self and other, we are able to truly appreciate the dignity of every human being. Christians welcome good works such as the admirable efforts of Doctors Without Borders. But Christian humanism does not reduce charity to a means of this-worldly transformation. The life of the soul as illustrated by Mother Teresa has "specifically Christian dimensions not found within humanitarianism."

I have concentrated on the insights of Pierre Manent in no small part because he is that rare contemporary who appreciates the defects of humanitarianism on political, philosophical, and theological grounds. He grasps the whole picture, so to speak. He is also that rare Christian who appreciates that Christians, too, are political animals, and not first and foremost "citizens of the world." Once an indispensable category of Aristotelian and Thomistic thought, the "common good" is increasingly identified by popes and other Christians in positions of authority with a nonexistent "world governing authority" (this unfortunate locution can be found in papal social encyclicals dating back to the 1960s). It is fair to say that Catholic thought has been infected by a humanitarian virus that forgets the wisdom of subsidiarity (the need to diffuse political and social power) and the fact that humanity is for many a self-conscious substitute for the Church as the "bearer and instrument of charity" for a humankind "wounded and divided by sin," to cite Manent again. Nor do the most influential teachers of the faithful fully appreciate that the "contemporary religion of humanity excludes and rejects the Christian religion." Global elites, mainly but not exclusively European, simply "believe in humanity," in human equality and resemblance; they do not see any need for the grace of which the Church is the indispensable sacramental instrument.

THE PASSIVITY OF CONTEMPORARY HUMANITARIANISM

Manent has also pointed out that contemporary humanitarianism is remarkably passive, allowing its adherents to detach themselves from the great "communities of action," such as nations and churches. Instead, they find salvation for themselves in strident affirmations of individual and collective autonomy, and not in deference to the grace and goodness of God. One of Manent's most striking insights is that the religion of humanity in its dominant forms is "not productive of community." Good works, humanitarian works, are welcomed, of course, but one can love Humanity through a vague and undemanding sentimentality. Loving real human beings is another matter altogether. It involves the exercise of the cardinal and theological virtues, which have little or no place in the new humanitarian dispensation. In its own way, humanitarianism is neither politically nor morally demanding. It makes the avant-garde of humanity feel smug and self-satisfied, needing neither grace nor the full exercise of the moral or civic virtues. It creates a world that has no place for either magnanimity, the supreme virtue of Plutarch's heroes or a Churchill or de Gaulle, or humility, the defining trait of Mother Teresa or St. Francis. Secular humanitarianism posits a world without heroes or saints, a world in which the capacity to admire what is inherently admirable is deeply undermined.

THE NEED FOR POLITICAL MEDIATION

Manent is both a Christian and an Aristotelian (he even says, once, "half-Thomist"). He has learned from Aristotle, the greatest political thinker, because he is the most discerning and the most sober, that the idea of man "is only able to realize itself in a particular political community." The world will always have many political communities (and most likely more than many). "Humanity" never has, and never will, exist as a real community. The Church is the only real universal community (if a spiritual one), even if empires from the Roman to the Soviet have aspired to universality. Like Aristotle, Manent denies that "humanity" can constitute a community without the "mediation of political institutions." In this world under the visible moon, the universal (human nature) is always mediated by the particular. This is not to deny the idea of a common humanity or the existence of moral obligations to those who live outside our political community, but Aristotle and Rousseau (who is no wide-eyed progressive on this issue) agree that a "reasonable" organization of the life of human beings depends upon promoting the common good of the political community in which we live. We do not live in the "world," even if nations and peoples ought to cooperate to promote goods that can never be fully achieved within a single political community (ecological issues come to mind here, as well as efforts at collective security on the part of free and civilized nations). And all evidence suggests that a world state would be a "soulless despotism," as Kant acknowledged in his 1795 work *Perpetual Peace*. Self-governing nations, especially of a "Christian mark," need not be animated by what Manent calls "homicidal aversion to their neighbors." That was the character and work of anti-Christian ideologies in the twentieth century. Our alternatives are by no means reducible to a thankless choice between "blood and soil" nationalism and work on behalf of a world community without particular political and spiritual bonds and attachments. In their own indispensable ways, nations embody shared human concerns and enliven vigorous and humane common life. They certainly need not be instruments of inhumanity or ethnic tribalism, as their critics falsely assert. Informed by the cardinal virtues, they can give rise to morally serious—prudent and humane—political action.

THE INDISPENSABILITY OF THE CARDINAL AND THEOLOGICAL VIRTUES

Manent provocatively suggests that of all religions, the religion of humanity "is easiest to show as being based on an illusion." To begin with, it is "a strictly European affair" (as it was in Comte's time) that is blind to the "precarious equilibrium determined by the political and spiritual decisions of human communities." To understand those decisions, and to take them oneself, one must recur to the lexicon and catalog "of the cardinal and theological virtues." Prudence, moderation, justice, and fortitude should continue to inform human thought and action as they have from the times of King David, Pericles, and St. Paul. These are the virtues one sees on display in Plutarch's *Lives* and in Shakespeare's Roman and English plays (this is one reason why liberal education, classical education, remains indispensable). Instead of self-satisfied humanitarian affirmations, we need citizenship and statesmanship that pursue the common good in a world of nations. We need to remember that virtue can take the form of a Lincoln, a Churchill, or a de Gaulle, magnanimous statesmen all, and not merely of a self-giving Mother Teresa. We must make more of an effort to see virtue in all its amplitude, in the person of the hero and the statesman as well as the saint. In the modern world, heroes and saints stand or fall together.

Instead of identifying the theological virtue of charity with inter-mundane humanitarianism, the Catholic Church ought to thoughtfully address "the propositions about humanity" put forward by the great religions and nations of the world, from Islam to China to evangelical Christianity, and the contemporary ideology of the rights of man. The goal ought not to be a facile ecumenism (or the denial of uncomfortable truths about Islam), but a "serious conversation" about the good of man that remains mindful of the ideological perversions that have deformed modernity. To pursue this great dialogue with the full array of nations, peoples, and religions, the Church must display both self-confidence and equanimity and a singular devotion to truth and to dialogue.

But this means that the Church must see totalitarianism and the religion of humanity for what they are, grave temptations that distort and subvert the true temporal and spiritual destinies of humankind. Manent also provocatively suggests that the Church can only recover a sense of her distinct role as the great Mediator of Divine Truth and Grace if she also recognizes the crucial mediating role of the nation as a mediator of a shared humanity. As he phrases it, "the effort of mediation is spiritual and political" and depends upon a recovery by Christians of an understanding of themselves as "political animals" (and thus the dignity of the nation) and not as citizens of some non-existent "world." To recover mediation is to recover the great insights of classical and Thomistic political philosophy, to take political philosophy as seriously as the Church now takes moral theology. Manent's work shows the way to this much needed recovery.

THE FULL RANGE OF REASON

Pope Benedict XVI was the last great churchman to fully appreciate the folly of humanitarianism and the positivism that lies behind it. He stood for the integrity of Reason, understood in a broadly classical and Christian sense. Against the proponents of "de-Hellenization," he defended the "inner rapprochement" between biblical faith and Greek philosophical inquiry, one that allowed reason to speak intelligibly about the Creative Reason or Logos at the source of the universe itself. The "self-imposed limitation of reason to the empirically falsifiable," Benedict suggested at Regensburg in the fall of 2006, crippled reason by confusing faith with fideism and confining reason to the realm of technological or instrumental rationality. Reason must relearn, however modestly or tentatively, to speak again about the soul and its encounter with God. Meanwhile, the liberal theology of the nineteenth century, represented by the likes of Adolf von Harnack, and by Bultmann in the twentieth, had promoted a too-radical divide between "the God of the philosophers" and the "God of Abraham, Isaac, and Jacob." In this view, Christianity was to be freed from the "accretions of theology" in which it found itself and from all Hellenistic influences, with worship of the Triune God to be replaced by a "humanitarian moral message" (of which Jesus was said to be the preeminent inspiration). Harnack did not promote human self-deification à la Comte, but he did crudely divorce biblical truth from meaningful transcendental reference points. His was among the first of many ideological reductions of Christian truth to something other than itself. In Harnack and his ilk, we find one of the most important theological sources of the humanitarian subversion of Christianity.

BENEDICT ON THE TEMPTATIONS OF CHRIST

Pope Benedict's critique of humanitarianism is perhaps best expressed in his luminous treatment of "The Temptations of Jesus" in the second chapter of the first volume of *Jesus of Nazareth*. The temptation stories in the Gospels of Matthew and Luke are recollections of an inner struggle in the soul of Christ. "Tempted by the devil" (*Matthew* 4:1), Jesus must struggle to remain faithful to his task and not be misled by the provocations and false promises of the Evil One. The Devil promises Christ political power and the amelioration of the "social problems" that plague humanity. Will Christ set God aside as an "illusion" that gets in the way of truly pressing problems, or will he remain faithful to the mission that his Father has entrusted to Him? The Devil imagines a world that human beings construct "by our own lights," without aid from the grace and goodness of the Eternal God. In this understanding, everything is to be reduced to the "political and the material," to an essentially ideological understanding of human life. This is what Christ in no uncertain terms rejects. Christianity can never be understood as a merely "humanitarian" project without betraying faith in the promises of God or a true understanding of Jesus's mission on Earth.

The pope emeritus shows what is at stake in the Devil's admonition to "Command this stone to become bread" (*Luke* 4:30). What an affront world hunger is! and how pressing this problem must appear to the One with a truly messianic vocation. Must not it—the provision of bread—"be the first test of the Redeemer, before the world's gaze and on the world's behalf, to give it bread and to end all hunger?" This is what Marxism would so clamorously demand in the nineteenth and twentieth centuries—a solution of the social problem, including hunger, before human beings could even begin to address concerns of the soul (if they indeed had souls). Give the people bread and then worry about virtue and freedom, Dostoevsky's Grand Inquisitor famously exclaimed. But Benedict highlights a great paradox: a materialist ideology such as Marxism led to hunger and starvation on a truly massive scale in Soviet Russia and Ukraine, Maoist China, Ethiopia, and North Korea. These were not the results of "bad weather," but rather were built into the very DNA of Marxism-Leninism. By ignoring the needs of the soul, by pushing to the side the inherent dignity of the human person, Marxism led to "ruin and destruction even of material goods themselves." "The most important things" are not material goods but the indelible fact that men and women are made in the image and likeness of God and must be treated accordingly. (It could be added that Marxism could not do justice to elementary self-interest either, even of the most natural and legitimate kind.) "The negative outcome of the Marxist experiment" proves that the Devil's path—the humanitarian's path—is the road to perdition. No social problems are so pressing that we should sacrifice human dignity and liberty in the effort to "solve" them immediately. The proper "ordering of goods" is a precondition for avoiding "ruin and destruction" on the spiritual *and* the material planes. With its primacy of the socially pressing, humanitarianism paradoxically sacrifices real human beings to what Pope Benedict elsewhere calls "the Moloch of the future."

Let us reiterate: if it is to remain true to itself, Christianity is not, and must not become, an ideological project. In the last temptation in the Gospels of both Matthew and Luke, in a vision the Devil takes the Lord to a high mountain. He "shows him all the kingdoms of the earth and their splendor and offers him kingship over the whole world." But the Incarnate Lord does not see his mission as one of establishing a humanitarian world-state. He resists the demonic temptation to become a "servant of power" and to bend to the requirements of a kingdom that loses sight of Almighty God and his purposes for humanity. Christ's kingdom is ultimately not of this world, even if the seeds of the kingdom (like the "mustard seeds" of the parables) are announced in multiple ways through Christ's preaching and miracles. Unlike Barabbas, Christ is no "robber," no "zealot," no freedom fighter. The salvation the Son of Man offers is not political liberation, not emancipation in this world from the terrible challenges of sin and death. His is a call to repentance and not a project to promote political "liberation." Pope Benedict is quite taken by the nineteenth-century Russian philosopher and theologian Vladimir Soloviev's portrait of the Antichrist, who announces with great fanfare the need to give priority "to a planned and organized world." Soloviev's Antichrist is a thoroughgoing humanitarian, as we shall see in Chapter Three—one who promises humankind a perverse "secular salvation" and a Kingdom without Christ the King.

THE FOLLY OF LIBERATION THEOLOGY

For all these reasons, Pope Benedict was a firm, if measured, critic of "liberation theology." He understood it as an ideological project that reduced Christianity to a vehicle for a reckless and inhuman version of political "emancipation." Uncritically appropriating Marxist social analysis, it transformed the Gospel's tension between the poor and "the poor in spirit" into a crude advocacy of "class struggle" where hate had primacy over love. It too often saw the Kingdom of God at work in malign tyrannies such as Mao's China and Castro's Cuba. Christians do indeed side with the poor, but not in any reductive ideological sense. All groups, all classes, suffer from inordinate self-regard and are prone to sin and selfishness. The poor in the modern world can be just as rapacious and power hungry as some of the rich. The poor as an ideological category, as privileged beneficiaries of transformative revolution (in any case, a hopelessly utopian concept), owe nothing to Christian revelation. As I will suggest later in this book, tens of millions of innocent human beings—kulaks, merchants, the bourgeoisie, aristocrats, religious believers, and independent thinkers of all sorts—were killed in the twentieth century in the name of proletarian revolution. The poor as an ideological category are a "temptation" put forward to undermine sensible political efforts on behalf of a common good that do justice to the rightful claims of *all* individuals and groups within decent political orders. One need only look at the sorry course of the Chavista revolution in Venezuela: law is under systematic assault, bread is absent from bakeries, the poor suffer terribly, the currency is degraded, and the middle classes are despoiled. And Pope Francis, too sympathetic to liberation theology, says nothing despite the repeated appeals of the Venezuelan bishops, who speak as the conscience of the nation. Pope Benedict repeatedly insisted that the program of the Good Samaritan should not be confused in any way whatsoever with the revolutionary agenda of *The Communist Manifesto*. There lay the comprehensive falsification of Christ's Gospel and a latter-day succumbing to the temptations of the Devil, the Evil One. Later, we shall explore that always-present demonic temptation with the help of Vladimir Soloviev, the author of the remarkably prescient *A Short Tale of the Antichrist* (1900).

"CARITAS" VERSUS HUMANITARIAN "LOVE"

One of Pope Benedict's most significant contributions is to remind Christians and all men of good will that egalitarian social justice will never replace the need for love—*caritas*—in the lives of men or in the social order more broadly. There will also be loneliness; there will always be those who suffer. The corporal works of mercy are essential, but "care of the soul" should always have pride of place; it "often is even more necessary than material support." Benedict makes this point clearly in his 2005 encyclical *Deus Caritas Est* (*God Is Love*). There he upholds the principle of subsidiarity and warns against an impersonal bureaucratic state usurping the responsibilities of citizens and believers. A humanitarianism that saps an energetic and morally serious civil society makes the world a less loving place, and almost certainly a more regimented one. Christian charitable activity must scrupulously avoid ideological cooptation and must never see its work as somehow buttressing an unjust society (an inhuman argument first put forward by Lenin). We are obliged "to act humanely here and now" and not to succumb to misplaced eschatological hopes of an inter-mundane character. Our program, the program of the Good Samaritan and Jesus Christ, is that of "a heart that sees" and not that of a humanitarian creed or secular messianism.

CONCLUSION

Pope Benedict provides indispensable guidance for avoiding both the revolutionary and humanitarian temptations, both at odds with the faith of Christ and with decent, prudent, and humane politics. The love that Benedict heralds is a love informed by divine caritas, and not a crude instrument at the service of human self-deification or the terrestrial self-satisfaction of the human race. As Benedict sees it, God's love opens the soul to what is above it and transforms it; Comte's love closes us to the transcendental sources of true human dignity. One is an impostor, the other the real thing. Humanitarianism as Comte first proclaimed it is an "idol" of the first order at the service of a soul-destroying illusion. In their different ways, Pierre Manent and Pope Benedict alert us to the multiple ways by which "the religion of humanity" subverts authentic love, undermines true "communities of action," and undermines the full range of the cardinal and theological virtues that come to view in free political life. The latter have nothing in common with the ideological projects that have deformed late modernity. Politics is preeminently the realm of prudence, a moral virtue that allows us to do justice to principle, and humane and calibrated judgment, in the rough and tumble of political life. The great Anglo-Irish statesman Edmund Burke, who so nobly embodied this virtue, went so far as to call it "the god of this lower world."

The Church can recover her own work of mediation only when she truly appreciates the humanitarian temptation for what it is: not the completion or perfection of the Christian ethic in the secular world, but a massive "falsification of the good," as Alain Besançon has put it, one that finally subverts all that is decent in the contemporary world and in the life of the faith. As we shall see in coming chapters, deeply insightful nineteenth-century

Christian thinkers such as Orestes Brownson and Vladimir Soloviev, an American and a Russian, respectively, had already uncovered, with rare depth and penetration, what was entailed in the humanitarian distortion of the good. It is to them that we turn in Chapters Two and Three.

• SOURCES AND SUGGESTED READINGS •

The epigram comes from Pierre Manent, "La tentation de l'humanitaire," *Géopolitique*, no. 68 (2000): p. 8. The early quotations from Manent are drawn from his treatment of Comte in *A World beyond Politics? A Defense of the Nation-State*, translated by Marc Le Pain (Princeton, NJ and Oxford: Princeton University Press, 2006), p. 125, and Pierre Manent, "Human Unity Real and Imagined," *First Things* (October 2012).

I have drawn extensively from August Comte, *System of Positive Polity*, Volume I, translated by John Henry Bridges (New York: Burt Franklin, 1875), especially the chapters "Intellectual Character of Positivism" and "Conclusion: The Religion of Humanity."

On the "inter-mundane eschatology" at the heart of Comte's reflection, see Eric Voegelin, "Apocalypse of Man: Comte" in Voegelin, *From Enlightenment to Revolution*, edited by John H. Hallowell (Durham, NC: Duke University Press, 1975), especially p. 157. On the substitution of altruism for *amor Dei*, see p. 155. On Mill's and Littre's break with Comte, see p. 142. On the absence of Christ from the *Calendrier*, see the chapter "The Religion of Humanity and the French Revolution" in *From Enlightenment to Revolution*, p. 161.

On Comte's expectation of the permanent abolition of war from the avant-garde of humanity, see the discussion in Raymond Aron, *Main Currents of Sociological Thought*, Volume I (New Brunswick, NJ: 1998), p. 90. See p. 304 for Aron's particularly helpful discussion of Comte's contempt for liberal or representative institutions.

On the religion of humanity as a form of fanaticism, see Pierre Manent, *Seeing Things Politically: Interviews with Benedicte Delorme-Montini*, trans. by Ralph C. Hancock, Introduction by Daniel J. Mahoney (South Bend, IN: St. Augustine's Press, 2015), pp. 151–152. On the contemporary contempt for "mediation," see *Seeing Things Politically*, p. 150.

See pp. 160–162 for Manent's discussion of the differences between Christianity and the religion of humanity, and between compassion and charity. I am also indebted to Manent's helpful discussion of Mother Teresa.

On the political community as a genuine "community of action," see Manent, "Human Unity Real and Imagined." See the same essay for a discussion of the passivity that accompanies "the religion of humanity." I am indebted to Manent's discussion of the indispensability of the lexicon of the cardinal and theological virtues.

On the profound difference between the "nation of the Christian mark" and the totalitarian nation that promotes "homicidal aversion" to other peoples and nations, see Manent, *Beyond Radical Secularism*, trans. by Ralph C. Hancock, Introduction by Daniel J. Mahoney (South Bend, IN: St. Augustine's Press, 2016), pp. 111–112.

On Aristotle's point that humanity only realizes itself in particular political communities, see Manent's discussion in *Géopolitique*, p. 8. See Manent, "Humanity Real and Imagined" for a luminous discussion of how only the Church can initiate a discussion among the great political and spiritual affirmations that animate humankind today.

I have drawn on Pope Benedict's "Regensburg Address" in *Liberating Logos: Pope Benedict's September Speeches*, edited by Marc D. Guerra (South Bend, IN: St. Augustine's Press, 2014), especially pp. 31–36. For an unsurpassed discussion of the temptations of Christ in the desert, see Pope Benedict, *Jesus of Nazareth*, translated by Adrian J. Walker (New York: Doubleday, 2007), especially pp. 28, 31, 33, and 41.

For Pope Benedict's critique of liberation theology, see his 1985 "Instruction on Liberation Theology" in *The Essential Pope Benedict: His Central Speeches and Writings*, edited by John F. Thornton and Susan B. Varenne (New York: HarperCollins, 2007), especially pp. 217, 221, 223. On the incompatibility of Christian love with ideological projects of all sorts, see *God Is Love* in *The Essential Pope Benedict*, pp. 415, 418–419.

CHAPTER TWO

Orestes Brownson: From the Religion of Humanity to Catholicism and Constitutional Republicanism

O restes Brownson is the preeminent American Catholic political thinker of the nineteenth century. Born in 1803, he converted to Catholicism in 1844 and remained a thoughtful and committed Catholic until his death in 1876. It is currently fashionable to see Brownson as a "weathervane," someone who simply reflected the diverse intellectual currents of his time. The poet James Russell Lowell wrote a famous verse about Brownson encapsulating this view: "He shifts quite about and then proceeds to expound/ That it's merely the earth, not himself, that turns around." But Peter Augustine Lawler has argued persuasively that "once Brownson became a Catholic, he did stop shifting," at least in any fundamental sense. "He was a seeker who finally found what he was looking for." From 1844 until 1876, writing in *The Brownson Quarterly Review*, this New Englander articulated a mature Catholic political philosophy that defended American republicanism on Catholic and natural law grounds. He self-consciously repudiated "the religion of humanity," going so far as to identify it as the source of his most egregious misjudgments before 1844. His is what Charles Péguy called a *cas éminent*, a particularly revealing case of a great mind and thinker who liberated himself from an early version of liberation theology and pantheistic humanitarianism. Along with the Russian philosopher and theologian Vladimir Soloviev (1853–1900), Brownson remains the deepest

Christian critic of everything entailed in the reduction of Christianity to mere humanitarianism.

This judgment is amply supported by a careful reading of Richard Reinsch's admirably comprehensive new anthology of Brownson's writings, *Seeking the Truth*, published by Catholic University Press in a handsome paperback volume in 2016. Covering 46 years (1827–1873), this 524-page volume gives contemporary readers access both to Brownson's best and most revealing writings and to his intellectual odyssey as a whole. As one critic has noted, Brownson is a "most interesting thinker, and a prolix writer." He writes clearly, at times elegantly, but with a marked tendency to repeat himself. Yet his thought forms a compelling whole, and Reinsch's volume allows one to fully measure his achievement. No mere weathervane, he was an indefatigable searcher for truth who believed he had found it after he converted to Catholicism. There would be no more wavering on the fundamentals, although some of his judgments on practical matters, and the best way to defend the faith, shifted in the decades before his death. In *The Convert*, a deeply informative memoir published in 1857 (now available in print again), Brownson attributed his conversion both to God's grace and to the fruitful workings of reason. His rejection of a godless rationalism in no way entailed a turn toward fideism or a sentimentality devoid of reason. For the mature Brownson, reason and revelation were full collaborators, revealing the whole truth about man and the essential nature and structure of reality. As a young man in the 1820s, Brownson had briefly turned to Presbyterianism, and attributed that short-lived conversion to a *repudiation* of reason. In becoming a Presbyterian, he had "despaired of reason" (*TC*, 229). He saw his affirmation of the Catholic religion, by contrast, as a vindication of both reason and truth. Catholicism, for Brownson, was incompatible with both hyper-rationalism and anything that smacked of a rejection of reason within its own legitimate sphere.

THE RELIGION OF HUMANITY

One of the central chapters of *The Convert* is entitled "The Religion of Humanity" (*TC*, 99–107). In the years before Brownson's conversion to the Catholic faith, he wandered from Congregationalism to Presbyterianism to Universalism to Unitarianism and Saint-Simonianism—with a famous overlapping five-year stint in Transcendentalism (1836 to 1841). In every stage of his early intellectual development (after Presbyterianism), Brownson remained a humanitarian who believed in "the creation of an earthly paradise" (*TC*, 81). His religion was devoid of any sense of transcendence. His essays from this period are studded with references to "illimitable progress" (*STT*, 148) and to the "regeneration" *(STT*, 98) of the American people and the human race. He told the famous historian George Bancroft that, in works such as *New Views of Christianity, Society, and the Church* (1836), he aimed to "democratize religion and philosophy" (See Reinsch's Introduction to *STT*, 9). His early writings are filled with paeans to the progress and redemptive transformation of the human race. Peter Lawler rightly characterizes him during this period as a "pantheist and gnostic" who believed that the Kingdom of God could be established on Earth.

The pre-Catholic Brownson saw no meaningful distinction whatsoever between the human and the divine. For him, the "Incarnation" revealed the truth of pantheism and must be understood in light of it. Yet he still felt compelled to present his progressivism in Christian terms. In "The Religion of Humanity," Brownson acknowledged that he was moved by "certain religious sentiments" that he could not "efface" (*TC*, 101 for all quotations in this paragraph). But in the end he "professed to hold no religion except that of humanity." "The only God" he recognized was "the Divine in Man." Such was the meaning of the "atonement" as Brownson then understood it. Jesus was divine only in the sense that all men are divine or are in the process of secular divinization: there was "nothing supernatural in his person and character." Jesus was essentially a social reformer trying to promote progress and the well-being of the human race. He was at best a model man, one possible exemplar of humanity. Brownson, "as a good Protestant," used the Bible for his own purposes. He freely passed over everything that a "progressive" humanity had obviously "overgrown." So even as a Saint-Simonian, upholding the religion of humanity, lauding "a new Christianity," affirming the clear superiority of a pacific industrial society to military and feudal orders, Brownson still called himself a Christian. Belief in humanity, in inevitable progress, in the self-deification of man was, for him, the heart of any viable Christianity for the modern world. Not yet appreciating that the self-deification of man led to his self-enslavement, Brownson actively subverted Christianity even as he thought he was completing it.

In his remarkable 1834 "Memoir of Saint-Simon," Brownson paid tribute to the founder of the religion of humanity. Nothing was fixed, he asserted, and divinity revealed itself only in the worship of what was highest in man (Auguste Comte would later develop in a much more systematic way the worship appropriate to the religion of humanity). Brownson came to stand for progress and a union of the spiritual and the temporal, the spiritual and the material. Such union thoroughly "immanentized" the spiritual longings of human beings (*STT*, 128). Like Claude-Henri Saint-Simon and his followers, Brownson identified religion with a version of socialism that did not entirely repudiate private property (although in his most radical essay, "The Laboring Classes" (*STT*, 162–189) from 1840, he would come very close to doing so). Devoid of a transcendent God, his Christianity also had no sense of the ineradicable reality of evil in the human condition. He differed from the Saint-Simonians only in arguing that their Christianity wasn't new, but was, in truth, the hidden meaning of Christianity from its inception. From 1834 to 1841, Brownson insisted that the religion of humanity was the effectual truth of Christianity.

The later Brownson would, of course, come to see the religion of humanity as the deadly enemy of Christian truth and of a genuinely free and republican order. As Reinsch points out in his thoughtful and ample Introduction to *Seeking the Truth*, the later Brownson followed Alexis de Tocqueville in seeing pantheism and the religion of humanity as the ultimate theoretical and practical challenge to freedom, rightly understood (*STT*, 22). True individuality must accept natural limits and human distinctiveness. It must also affirm the freedom and sovereignty of God, a freedom that has nothing to do with arbitrariness or despotism of any sort. Human beings are "relational" beings who live in communion with others. But they also can only commune with God through the mediation of the Savior Jesus Christ (*STT*, 193–223). To conflate God, man, and the universe is to destroy the rights of God and the rights of man, to eliminate the very grounds of human distinctiveness and responsibility. Brownson came to this awareness by 1842, with help from the writings of Pierre Leroux. Leroux, no Christian, taught him the importance of human "communion" with God, nature, and other human beings. By 1842, Brownson had concluded that there could be no progress in the world without the sustenance of a Creator God. This was the beginning of Brownson's rejection of a facile faith in historical progress.

THE TURN TO CONSTITUTIONAL REPUBLICANISM

Brownson's movement toward political, philosophical, and theological sanity probably would not have occurred without the jarring events associated with the election of 1840. He saw that his endorsement of class struggle in "The Laboring Classes," his celebrated essay from 1840, was used by the Whigs against Martin van Buren and the Democrats, his preferred candidate and party, in the election of that year. He later came to see that his own "horrible doctrines" (as he called them in *The Convert*, 137–147) were used against an able and public-spirited candidate in the one election he actively participated in. He became "disgusted' with democracy, but not with "Constitutional Republicanism" (*TC*, 161) as he called it. Liberty, he came to understand, "is not in the absence of authority, but in being held to obey only just and legitimate authority" (*TC*, 161). Reading Aristotle's *Politics* for the first time, he learned a more serious and sober way of reflecting on the common good and the limits of mass democracy. He now thought about politics in the light of philosophy and experience and not utopian aspirations.

This movement from progressivist assumptions culminated in his great 1844 essay "Demagoguism," which is included in Reinsch's anthology. Brownson there defended republican government while opposing "the democratic principle," at least in its most absolutist or "willful" forms. He came to believe that popular government depended "on the virtue and intelligence of the people" and thus on fixed standards of immutable justice that were not the product of some unfolding and progressive historical process. He believed that in his lifetime the American polity had become more of a democracy and less of a republic, thereby largely repudiating the more demanding civic virtues. He now appealed to "Eternal Justice" and to the moral virtues, including "stern integrity," that were required of the rich and poor alike (*STT*, 236–237). And his political thinking had now become infused with Orthodox Christian and Aristotelian categories. By 1845 the newly converted Brownson had concluded, in his first great piece of political philosophizing written after his conversion, that "Catholicity [Was] Necessary to Sustain Popular Liberty" (*STT*, 241–255).

ROMAN CATHOLICISM AND POPULAR LIBERTY

In a confident and assertive tone, Brownson made a formidable argument
for the place the Roman Catholic religion could play in sustaining popular
liberty. Catholicism was a religion "free from popular control," a religion
that could uphold "truth, piety, moral and social virtue" in a way that
was immune from the willfulness or misplaced sovereignty of the people.
"It was not made by the people, but for them; is administered not by the
people, but for them; is accountable not to the people, but to God" (STT,
251). At the same time, Brownson made no claims for the "political power"
(STT, 253) of the Church. For the rest of his life he would defend popular
government while arguing, as he did in The American Republic (1865), that
popular sovereignty is legitimate only in a secondary or "derivative" sense:
all authority is ultimately "under God" (STT, 472).

Even in his most conservative affirmations, Brownson argued only for
the "moral authority" (STT, 253) of the Church in shaping the character,
ideas, and aspirations of a democratic people. He was, and would remain, a
passionate opponent of "clerocracy" (STT, 370–371) or clerical government
in all its forms. Brownson's "Catholicity Necessary to Sustain Popular
Government" makes this argument with considerable eloquence: "The only
influence on the political or governmental actions of the people which we
seek from Catholicity, is that which it exerts on the mind, heart, and the
conscience;—an influence it exerts by enlightening the mind to see the
true end of man, the relative value of all worldly pursuits, by moderating
passions, by weaning the affections from the world, inflaming the heart
with true charity, and by making each act in all things seriously, honestly,
conscientiously" (STT, 253). The Church should seek no political dominion.
Rejecting both theocratic temptation and moral indifferentism, Brownson
placed his hopes in the voluntary adherence of a free people to religious
truth and natural justice.

Brownson always remained faithful to this "liberal" commitment to
religious and political liberty and to his fervent opposition to every form
of clerical interference in free political life. But his Catholic liberalism was
always accompanied by a "conservative" opposition to the "revolutionary spirit" that he believed was fatal to a well-constituted democracy. He
would henceforth associate revolution and the revolutionary spirit with
"insubordination" and "disorder" (STT, 255). Once a partisan of "illimitable

progress," he now affirmed the necessity of "fixed rules" (*STT*, 255). He applauded Catholicism for its "immobility" at the level of truth—"all else may change, but it changes not" (*STT*, 255). It is a mirror of "the immobility and immutability of the eternal God." The human will must *freely* subordinate itself to eternal justice and enduring truth. This is the task of an authentic Christian republicanism: to sustain what Brownson's contemporary Alexis de Tocqueville once called, in *The Old Regime and the Revolution*, "liberty under God and the laws." Without deference to natural justice, democracy unleashes the predations of the strong and the moral anarchy of the untutored masses.

In an important 1849 essay on "Authority and Liberty," Brownson clarifies the relations between "the rights of God" and "the rights of Man." When God's sovereignty is attacked, our rights are undermined, "for all human rights are summed up in the one right to be governed by God and by him alone, in the duty of absolute subjection to him, and absolute freedom from subjection to any other" (*STT*, 269). As Lawler has noted, Brownson knowingly repudiated the Lockean idea of human "self-ownership." We have no right to own or tyrannize others, because we do not truthfully own ourselves. Men are fundamentally dependent on God and society, not on themselves. We are not autonomous beings. Brownson is a Catholic who does not believe in a willful or voluntaristic God in the manner of Islam or extreme versions of Calvinism. In his authentically Catholic conception, God is not a despot. Rather, his power is always accompanied by justice, his will by reason. "His sovereignty is rightful, his will is intrinsically, eternally, and immutably just will, his power just power. There is no opposition or tension between the divine will and natural justice: absolute subjection to him is absolute subjection to eternal, immutable, and absolute justice" (*STT*, 270). Brownson is both a theist and a defender of natural right—and for him these two affirmations go hand in hand. He helps us recover a notion of authority that is wholly distinct from arbitrariness or authoritarianism, and his orthodox theology provides a fertile ground for non-despotic politics and a conception of religion divorced from all fanaticism.

TRUE AND FALSE LIBERALISM AND CONSERVATISM

In essays such as "Liberalism and Socialism" (1855) and "Civil and Religious Liberty" (1863), Brownson elucidated an admirably dialectical attitude toward modern liberalism. He opposed its excesses, at least in part, on philosophical and religious grounds. But he also made clear that he had no objection whatsoever to parliamentary or constitutional government. He faulted the Spanish Catholic philosopher and doctrinaire Donoso Cortés for transforming a perfectly persuasive critique of humanitarianism into a thoroughgoing critique of constitutional government. That was another matter altogether (*STT*, 344–346). The great error of "European liberalists" was, in Brownson's view, less political than religious: their refusal to acknowledge the sovereignty of God as the basis of non-despotic politics (*STT,* 347). He found no fault in them for placing their hopes in "checks and balances" and government by compromise—these were admirable contrivances of prudence that did much to support a regime of liberty (*STT*, 347). He acknowledged that the liberal and socialist revolutions of Europe, beginning with the French revolution of 1789 and continuing through the revolutions of 1848, had "philanthropic" and humanitarian origins (at least in part) rather than merely destructive ones (*STT*, 351). Modern revolutionaries were responding to genuine injustices and could not be condemned *tout court.* Of course, their humanitarianism was itself problematic. Brownson had lost all confidence in "philanthropy, when acting alone, to effect anything good, for it seldom fails to make matters worse" (*STT*, 353).

Still, his passionate opposition to the modern revolutionary spirit did not make Brownson indulgent to the reactionary rejection of constructive change or reform. He firmly differentiated authentic conservatism from the "shallow and selfish declamations" (*STT*, 353) of those who merely defended the status quo. The "only conservatism" (*STT*, 353) he could respect was one that acknowledged social and political evils and did its best to redress them by all available non-revolutionary means. He could not tolerate systematic misgovernment or the neglect of the poor. Modern revolution of an ideological cast "was no fitting remedy" *(STT,* 353) for the evils that afflicted France on the eve of the French Revolution. Nonetheless, the party of order needed to appreciate that social evils can grow beyond "reasonable endurance" (*STT*, 353) and that the privileged had an obligation to contribute to the common good, to a political order that respected the needs of the rich and the poor alike. The revolutionary principle was inhuman. But the toleration of systematic injustices in the name of preserving the existing order was nearly equally so. In the best liberal conservative tradition, Brownson was a conservative because he was a reformer, and he was a reformer because he wished to preserve the patrimony of civilization and a common good worthy of free men. He adamantly opposed the extremes of radical democracy, untrammeled oligarchy, and impious revolutionary despotism.

Brownson was also a fiery critic of the "oscurantisti" in the Church, those "obscurantists" who persisted "in governing men as children" (*STT*, 383). They falsely maintained that human beings should be kept in "perpetual childhood" (*STT*, 383), devoid of those responsibilities that allow them to live as free men and women. These small-minded men confused the sovereignty of God with clerical rule and forgot that God's representatives must relate to others as "pastors"—not lords or despots (*STT*, 383). The Church should cultivate the "freedom, intelligence…and moral convictions" (*STT*, 383) of Christians worthy to live in a free society. "Error" may have no moral rights (*STT*, 375), but it should have the same rights as the true faith when it comes to the exercise of religious liberty in a liberal society that respects the conscience of free human beings.

However, religious liberty must never become an excuse for political domination by the "enemies of religion" (*STT*, 387). A free society depends upon respect for the primacy of conscience and the natural moral law. When the state is used as an instrument of "infidelity" (*STT*, 387), "political atheism" (*STT*, 406) rules and religion is suppressed. This can take the form of the virulent atheistic totalitarianism that ravaged the twentieth century or more subtle "secularist" efforts to make infidelity the state religion. Liberalism can be a great force upholding civil and religious liberty, and thus human dignity, against enemies religious and non-religious. At the same time, Brownson appreciated that the liberal movement has always been haunted by "irreligion and infidelity" (*STT*, 407). When liberalism actively repudiates conscience and God, it turns against itself and becomes "incompatible with the salvation of souls and the progress of society" (*STT*, 407). Brownson is that rare political thinker who can teach us how to distinguish true from false liberalism and true from false conservatism. Moreover, he shows us how we can affirm the legitimacy of both liberalism and conservatism by recognizing their limits in light of the truth, natural justice, and the common good.

SLAVERY AND THE SOUTH

Brownson's judicious mixture of conservatism and liberalism is nowhere more apparent than in his attitude toward slavery and the American South. A fervent defender of the Union during the Civil War, he opposed slavery on moral, philosophical, and religious grounds. He advocated emancipation as a wartime measure that would aid the cause of union and liberty. He believed that secession was a deeply subversive act rooted in individualist premises that undermined the very possibility of ordered liberty. But he was no radical Republican. He did not wish to "New-Englandize" the South, to industrialize it beyond recognition, or to exterminate the Southern leaders. He admired many features of Southern life, its Stoic ideal and its gentlemanly traditions, even as he wished "to see the free-labor system substituted for the slave-labor system" (*STT*, 402). The cause of union and liberty was for Brownson a preeminently conservative one that defended the orderly national framework that was the precondition of all true liberty and all true federalism. Slavery was a moral abomination, but there were better and worse ways of eliminating this stain from the American body politic. Brownson's arguments are reminiscent of Burke's defense of traditional liberty (and his opposition to the oppression of Irish Catholics and the people of India) rather than the more "Jacobin" strain of northern Republicanism. Here, once again, we see the conservative as reformer. Whether one could truly conserve Southern traditions without the slave principle was a question Brownson never truly considered. But his writings show that one can fervently oppose injustice while rejecting the subversive spirit that informs modern revolution.

THE AMERICAN REPUBLIC AND TERRITORIAL DEMOCRACY

Brownson's "conservative" defense of American republicanism is most evident in *The American Republic*. Published in 1865, this classic work accepts "universal suffrage in principle" and defends American democracy against the twin extremes of "pure individualism on the one hand," and "from pure socialism or humanitarianism on the other" (*STT*, 421). The originality of this enduring work is rooted in its challenge to the social contract theory that, for better or worse, had become part of the "political tradition of the country" (*STT*, 445). Brownson believed that it was based on a voluntarism that ultimately undermined true liberty and true obedience. Contrary to the democratic dogma, Brownson repudiated the idea that the people have "divine" authority—they are in no way "independent, self-existing, and self-sufficing" (*STT*, 449). The people can only act as "a second cause," never as the "first cause" of their being and destiny (*STT*, 461). Brownson rejected "absolute sovereignty" and the emancipation of the human will from divine or natural superintendence. Only in recognizing our fundamental dependence on an order of Being outside ourselves can human liberty and dignity be sustained.

Brownson opposed Jeffersonian democracy's assertion of a pure individualism (not always self-consciously), which has no grounds for rejecting the utterly fallacious claim that human beings are gods (*STT*, 445–452). In particular, "pure egoism" undermines the loyalty and duty at the foundation of citizenship. Without the subordination of the self to what is outside and above it, a democracy ceases to be a true republic dedicated to the common weal or common good. It gives rise to unrestrained oligarchy and various manifestations of moral anarchy. The Catholic contribution to American republicanism is rooted in its capacity to give a credible natural law foundation to the rights and obligations of free men and women. American practice must be protected from a misplaced theory (social contractualism of the sort proffered by Hobbes, Locke, and Rousseau) that undermines all the legitimate aspirations of the American people to a dignified and ordered liberty.

If Brownson opposed rooting a constitutional republic in the collective will of the people, he never denied the moral and political agency of a free people deliberating about its future. He had carefully studied and drew considerable insights from Joseph de Maistre's 1809 work *Essay on the Generative Principle of Political Constitutions*, a ferociously anti-revolutionary work that denied the possibility of creating a political or constitutional order *de novo* or all at once (*STT*, 471–472). Unlike Maistre, however, Brownson never denied the possibility of a political founding such as the one that occurred in America in 1787. Not all foundings were willful, immoderate, or "revolutionary." The important thing was to avoid undue abstractions and to root a political founding, and a written constitution, in the "providential constitution" (*STT*, 477) of a people and nation. Free people like the American people were a "territorial democracy" with distinct traditions and habits that must inform true self-government. Such attentiveness to the inherited and territorial would protect a constitution from what was unduly "theoretic" and "unreal" (*STT*, 478). Brownson steadfastly insisted that only the "concrete is real," and "only the real or actual has vitality or force." "Constitutions conceived by philosophers in their closets are constitutions only of Utopia or Dreamland" (*STT*, 478). The American Founders—with their attention to history and experience and respect for the best traditions of the country, including the "rights of Englishmen"—could not be accused of utopian dreaming. Their founding was no "year zero," no attempt to break absolutely and definitively with the past. A spirit of moderation, not uninformed by classical prudence, guided their deliberations. In decisive respects, it might be said that their work was better than some of the theories that informed it. Brownson provides a salutary correction of a founding well worth preserving, a more consistent and true natural law foundation for free government. Brownson wrote as a Catholic, a republican, and a patriot, a man who cherished the best traditions of his country and who was driven by a passionate yet measured commitment to ordered liberty.

Territorial democracy, as Brownson conceived it, entails a liberty rooted in what Lawler aptly calls a "people's attachment to the soil." It is distinct from "personal authority," which gives rise to "barbarism" or despotism. As Peter Lawler notes, "the territorial principle is the foundation of all distinctively political authority." Richard Reinsch highlights an important passage in *The American Republic* where Brownson notes that the movement in the United States from the territorial principle to the affirmation of the "purely popular basis" of rule entails nothing less than the transformation of a "republican to a despotic, or from a civilized to a barbaric constitution" (quoted in *STT*, 32). Brownson rejected "the limitless claims of modern sovereignty" in the name of an understanding of "law, obligation, and right being fixed to a territory where it is exercised as a public trust" (Reinsch in *STT*, 32). This is the framework or body that actualizes consent within its legitimate sphere.

As we have seen, for Brownson, consent is always marked by limits and accompanying responsibilities. Liberty is always circumscribed and never "global" or "humanitarian." Such humanitarianism is woefully abstract and is too often coextensive with Dreamland. Territorial democracy is the liberty of *this* particular people, under *this* written and providential constitution. The nation is the political form of a liberty worthy of the name. It affirms universal moral obligations in a reasonable, circumscribed, and truly humane political context. In his magisterial "Introduction" to the 2003 re-edition of *The American Republic* published by ISI Books, Lawler draws suggestive parallels between Brownson's defense of "humane national loyalty" (Roger Scruton's phrase) and those put forward by Tocqueville, Charles de Gaulle, and the "French Catholic Tocquevillian" Pierre Manent.

All defended the "territorial" basis of republican government where "loyalty more than consent must be the foundation of free government and political life." All sensed that the depoliticization of modern democracy, in the name of individualist and humanitarian abstractions, went hand in hand with its deChristianization.

Today, we see that dynamic working itself out in a contemporary Europe that is depoliticizing and deChristianizing at an alarming rate. Such a Europe no longer acknowledges what Pierre Manent calls its "Christian mark." To truly defend what is "common," a free people needs to judiciously conjugate universality and particularity, loyalty and consent. A false and deceptive cosmopolitanism, which accompanies modern humanitarianism like a siren call, substitutes abstract claims for the demanding requirements of true citizenship. It apes the "universalism" of Christianity even as it distorts it beyond recognition. Like all Catholic and genuinely republican defenders of humane national loyalty, Brownson appreciated that human beings are not forced to choose between "pure socialism or humanitarianism" or "homicidal aversion" to other peoples or nations (the phrase, once again, is Pierre Manent's). In so doing, he helps us to think about the political forms appropriate to moderation and political liberty.

DEMOCRACY VERSUS THE "DEMOCRATIC PRINCIPLE"

Seeking the Truth culminates in the 1873 essay "The Democratic Principle," a striking restatement of Brownson's enduring themes, although cast in a somewhat more conservative or pessimistic light. Brownson reaffirms his long-standing commitment to "republican" government that is "largely popular in its constitution and administration" (*STT,* 499). But now he is absolutely forthright in his repudiation of the "democratic principle," more forthright than at any time in the past. He associates that principle with unbridled willfulness and the belief in the merely "conventional" origin of political authority. It explicitly rejects the *jus gentium*, the law of nations, and "the rule of eternal and immutable right." Conventionalism, or contractualism, the idea that political authority has no natural or divine authority other than human agreement, can place no limits on the arbitrary will of the few or the many. It inexorably leads to "government by force." It also provides no obstacle to Gallicanism, the idea repudiated by the First Vatican Council of 1870–71, that secular government ought to control episcopal appointments and the internal operations of the Church. As such it is incompatible with authentic religious liberty. In this last great essay, Brownson restates his adamant opposition to humanitarian democracy and political atheism.

Throughout this essay, Brownson shows that he is no "monarchist" or "revolutionary" and no enemy of republican government (*STT*, 501). He has no interest whatsoever in "warring against the political constitution" of his country. But he believes that the American constitutional order must defer to enduring "principles of law and justice" and not to the "democratic principle, which asserts the sovereignty of the arbitrary will of the people, or practically, the unrestricted rule of the majority for the time" (*STT*, 501). This is nothing less than tyranny and is "repugnant to the very essence of liberty, which is ruled by right, or power controlled by justice" (*STT*, 501). Brownson criticizes the democratic principle in the name of both political liberty and natural justice, two goods perfectly congruent with his Catholic faith. He is anti-democratic only if democracy means the emancipation of the human will in the name of untrammeled human self-sovereignty.

As we have stressed throughout this chapter, the task of Christian constitutionalism has nothing to do with the defense of clerical rule. Rather, it aims to free republican government from its "corruption" (the term is Montesquieu's) at the hands of a doctrine incompatible with the idea of the *res publica*, or the common weal or common good. The democratic principle has no place for a common good that mediates between the conflicting claims of the few and the many and the rich and the poor. At best, it follows Jeremy Bentham in defending "the greatest happiness of the greatness number" and does so on the simple grounds of utility. It excludes "the divine order from the state" (not to be confused with clerical or theocratic government) as well as "all rule of right" and of anything that is "eternal and immutable" (*STT*, 505). It thus provides no ground for resisting tyranny or the "triumph of the will" in any of its forms. It is a badly concealed form of moral nihilism and one that cannot endure over time.

Brownson is thus a friend of popular government (that commitment never wavered after 1844), but an implacable foe of a conception of democracy that divinizes the human will and reduces the origin of free government to an illusory social contract that empties citizenship of its moral content. This is the conundrum for a Catholic patriot who is also a constitutional republican: American principles, to the extent that they are indebted to social contract theory, slowly but surely undermine the genuine good at the heart of American constitutionalism. Constitutional republicanism, once again, is for Brownson founded on the sure foundation of the "regulated will," or "liberty under God."

Brownson had little faith in abstract declamations of political equality. As the 1873 essay makes clear, he believed that the emancipation of the human will would primarily benefit the "stronger interests," which are almost always the "business interests of the country" (*STT*, 506). Political atheism, which is the heart and soul of the democratic or humanitarian principle, excludes the moral element, founds the state on utility, and "tends to materialize the mind" (*STT*, 506). As Tocqueville also observed, it creates "a passion for sensible goods, or material wealth and well-being" (*STT*, 506). Brownson's critique of the democratic principle never leads to a complacent conservatism. America had become more oligarchic over time. Paradoxically, the "democratic principle" unleashed the increasingly unconstrained influence of the powerful and the rich. The contemporary relevance of this ought to be clear enough: the domination of the powerful and ambitious flows from democracy's founding premises, which over time undermines self-limitation and the wellsprings of moral obligation. It cannot be corrected on the basis of the "democratic principle" alone.

We should note that Brownson also believed that "equality in material goods" is not only an "impossibility" but an "absurdity" (*STT*, 508–509). Equality in material goods would create "equality in poverty." It would destroy the material preconditions of a free society. The "crimes" and "sacrileges" of the Communists deliver only misery and tyranny, while corrupting the human soul beyond recognition. Moreover, "all projects of reform of any sort, undertaken without divine authority, inevitably defeat themselves, and aggravate the evils they would address." Brownson foresaw all the evils associated with Communist totalitarianism in the twentieth century. He would have no sympathy for liberation theology or Christian Marxism in its various forms; in fact, he devastatingly dissected them *avant la lettre*. Like Péguy, he saw poverty as a dignified and holy thing, while lamenting the material and spiritual "misery" that many poor people, especially the poorest of the poor, experienced in ostensibly free and prosperous societies. But Christianity, properly understood, has nothing to do with dogmatic egalitarianism. It sees poverty itself as an instrument of holiness. Brownson made all the right distinctions and remains a sure guide for a Catholic republicanism that rejects the twin extremes of radical individualism (and the oligarchy that naturally stems from it) and socialist or revolutionary collectivism. He appreciated that strident demands for "social justice" were rooted in a materialist conception of human nature and society that is alien to authentic Christianity.

Despite his adamant rejection of the ever more ascendant "religion of humanity" with its divinization of the democratic principle, Brownson never lost hope in America. At the end of the 1873 essay, he expressed confidence that young Catholic men and women could renew an American republic worthy of the name. Counting on their moral efforts and their considerable public spiritedness, he did his best to educate his fellow Catholics and Americans (his audience and readership never simply consisted of his co-religionists). Near the end of "The Democratic Principle," he succinctly summarizes its moral and political lesson: "Now, it is easy to see that what we object to is not popular government, but the doctrine that the people as the state or nation are the origin of all authority and all law, that they are absolutely supreme and bound by no law or authority that does not emanate from themselves" (STT, 514). This is the heart and soul of humanitarian democracy and political atheism, of godless liberty. While his tone may have become more emphatic or "conservative" at the end of his life, Brownson was in fact still saying what he had repeated since his conversion to Catholicism in 1844 and his reading of Aristotle's Politics at about the same time. Like Tocqueville, Brownson is one of American democracy's "friendly critics." He, too, knew that philosophical modernity could not ultimately sustain a popular government that remained true to the requirements of "eternal justice." One must turn to older and richer spiritual resources in order to renew American republicanism and the democratic world more broadly.

CONCLUSION

I have tried to suggest just how instructive Orestes Brownson's intellectual, political, and religious odyssey is to all those who love free politics and who wish to recover the moral foundations of democracy. He came to appreciate that humanitarianism and political atheism would subvert both true Christianity and republican government committed to political liberty and the preservation of the common good. His own intellectual journey led him from the "horrible doctrines" discussed earlier in this chapter to a recovery of what we used to call, following both Cicero and the Catholic tradition, natural law and "right reason." We can be grateful for an experience that Brownson describes so well in *The Convert* in 1857, 13 years after his conversion: Listening to some lectures by Theodore Parker in the autumn of 1841, he heard "nothing except a learned and eloquent statement of the doctrine [he] had long defended, and which [he has] called the Religion of Humanity." But this time, something in Brownson's soul revolted against this reckless demand for human self-deification. For the first time, he "felt an invincible repugnance to it, and saw, or thought (he) saw at a glance, that it was unphilosophical and anti-religious" (*TC*, 201). This was a moment when grace met right reason. It sent Brownson on the path that he would so constructively follow until his death in 1876.

At the end of his introduction to his luminous anthology, Richard Reinsch observes that Brownson's "conversion from pseudosocialism and his American liberation theology" was rooted in the "freedom of God to create and sustain his creation" (*STT*, 35). The "rights of God," the sovereignty of God, are the only firm foundation for the "rights of man." As we have noted, Brownson's God, the God of Orthodox Christian theology, is no voluntaristic potentate. His will is always in accord with justice and reason. When we bow to Him, we say no to every form of human subjugation. Brownson was one of the first to see that "the humanitarian, therapeutic spirit" recognizes "no principled limits to its reformative power" (*STT*, 35). Rejecting the pantheism and human self-sovereignty he had earlier affirmed, Brownson came to place his faith in a loving, just, and relational God "who provides real support for human freedom and individuality" (*STT*, 35) rooted in the common good. For all these reasons, this unjustly neglected American political philosopher very much remains our much needed contemporary.

• SOURCES AND SUGGESTED READINGS •

The Works of Orestes A. Brownson were collected in 20 volumes by his son Henry F. Brownson and self-published by 1887. The most enduring and significant of those writings are collected in Richard M. Reinsch II's invaluable anthology *Seeking the Truth: An Orestes Brownson Anthology* (Washington, DC: Catholic University of America Press, 2016). His "Introduction" to that work has been very helpful. All quotations from that volume are published in the body of the text with the page numbers following *STT*. See Scott Yenor's excellent review of *Seeking the Truth* at www.claremont.org (June 28, 2017) for the remark about Brownson as "a most interesting thinker, and a prolix writer."

I was first seriously introduced to Brownson's significance as a political thinker by Peter Lawler's invaluable book-length "Introduction" to Brownson's *The American Republic* (Wilmington, Delaware, ISI Books, 2003). See p. LXXXXII for a helpful discussion of Brownson's constancy as a Catholic thinker, p. XIV for Lawler's discussion of Brownson's early pantheism and Gnosticism, and pp. XXIV–XXV for a lucid account of his repudiation of the Lockean idea of "self-ownership." I am also indebted to Lawler's account of Brownson's attitude toward the South and slavery, pp. XVII, and to his clarifications of what Brownson means by "territorial democracy," pp. XLII–XLIII.

I came across Brownson's *The Convert: Or, Leaves from My Experience* (1857) late in my work on this study. It is now available in an excellent edition edited by Arie J. Griffioen (Milwaukee, Wisconsin: Marquette University Press, 2012). This edition is cited internally in the text as *TC* followed by page numbers. This autobiographical account most helpfully highlights Brownson's movement away from "the religion of Humanity" after 1842.

For a lucid philosophical account of the "regulated will" as the basis of true political authority and true citizenship, see Bertrand de Jouvenel, *Sovereignty: An Inquiry into the Political Good* (Indianapolis, Indiana: Liberty Fund, 1997), pp. 238–257.

See p. III of Pierre Manent, *Beyond Radical Secularism: How France and the Christian West Should Respond to the Islamic Challenge*, translated by Ralph C. Hancock, Introduction by Daniel J. Mahoney (South Bend, Indiana: St. Augustine's Press, 2016) for an indispensable account of how "the nation understood as exclusive valorization of one's own people and homicidal aversion for people from elsewhere has little to do with the political form within which Europe arose and deployed its material and spiritual powers."

CHAPTER THREE

Soloviev on the Antichrist or the Humanitarian Falsification of the Good

In conclusion: Soloviev was undoubtedly a prophet and a teacher, but a teacher who was, in a way, irrelevant. And this, paradoxically, is why he was great and why he is precious for our time.

A passionate defender of the human person and allergic to every philanthropy; a tireless apostle of peace and adversary of pacifism; a promoter of Christian unity and critic of every irenicism, a lover of nature and yet very far from today's ecological infatuations—in a word, a friend of truth and an enemy of ideology.

— THE LATE GIACOMO CARDINAL BIFFI, ARCHBISHOP OF BOLOGNA

A masterpiece of world literature, Vladimir Soloviev's *A Short Tale of the Antichrist* is perhaps the most powerful and profound exploration of the humanitarian subversion of Christianity ever written. As Czesław Miłosz ably put it in an introduction to a 1990 edition of *War, Progress, and the End of History: Three Conversations*, "Soloviev provides what is seemingly impossible: a truly credible biography of that sublime and arresting Superman, the Anti-Christ. He conveys his powerful beauty, his spiritual powers, his claims to bring paradise to earth."

Representative of the last period of his thought, the *Short Tale* appeared shortly before Soloviev's untimely death at the age of 47 in 1900. The fruit of a mind that had ripened into deep maturity, the *Short Tale* reveals a thinker who saw the world unfolding before him with prophetic intensity, a prophetic intensity informed by immense learning and the soundest practical judgment. One cannot help but be impressed by the breadth and depth of Soloviev's theological, philosophical, and political reflection. Soloviev is well known as an advocate of Sophiology.

Soloviev's admirer and student Sergius Bulgakov, a Russian priest and a great Russian religious thinker in his own right, developed the tenets of Sophiology in the first part of the twentieth century. Soloviev's *Three Meetings* (1898) provides a poignant account of the three encounters (1862, 1875, and 1876) that Soloviev had with "Lady Wisdom" in Moscow, London, and Egypt, respectively. He experienced the radiance of "the eternal feminine," which he identified with the "Wisdom" mentioned in scripture. Some have criticized Sophiology as too gnostic and neo-platonic, or questionably Christian. But Soloviev strove, not always successfully, to keep his understanding of Sophia firmly within the bounds of Christian orthodoxy. Soloviev's heart and soul oscillated between mysticism and philosophy, between orthodoxy and theosophical speculation.

Soloviev is also well known for his *Lectures on Godmanhood* (1877–1884). Soloviev believed that humankind was capable of attaining deification, a union with the Creator God through the mediation of Christ Jesus and the Holy Spirit. Salvation entailed the restoration of all mankind, an eschatological process of becoming "divine." One might expect such an understanding of *Godmanhood* to be part and parcel of a larger progressivist, or historicist, or utopian political teaching. And, for a long time, Soloviev remained committed to the idea of a "free theocracy" in Russia and elsewhere. But he had an acute sense of the power of evil, especially in his later years. That sense is put on display in *A Short Tale of the Antichrist*. Soloviev gradually came to see that the moral optimism of the Enlightenment woefully understated the power of evil on the human, political, and eschatological plains. Following a youthful flirtation with leftist and revolutionary politics, he definitively rejected socialism and revolution.

In particular, Soloviev gave a balanced account of the nation and cosmopolitanism. A critic of what he perceived to be chauvinistic nationalism, he believed that cosmopolitanism ignored one of the fundamental traits of the human person: the flourishing of the human soul within a national framework. As Soloviev states in his beautiful 1895 essay "Nationality from a Moral Point of View," "Nationality is not only a physical fact, it is one of the most important positive traits of humankind." Soloviev defended what he saw as an authentically Christian principle, one that was necessary for true national health and self-consciousness. What he called "the moral point of view" thus transcended both nationalism and cosmopolitanism, while still managing to preserve "what is positive in them." During an age when intellectuals were obsessed with the idea of leaving national self-government behind in the name of an untenable cosmopolitan unity of the human race, he limned a Christian approach that responded (and ultimately overcomes) the dual excesses of both nationalism and cosmopolitanism. In this regard, he undoubtedly remains our contemporary.

Soloviev's appreciation of the power of evil is an important and necessary corrective to a moral optimism and historical progressivism that takes for granted the self-sufficiency of humankind and the self-evident goodness of a historical process that eschews justice and the providence of God. An immensely learned man who had translated Plato into Russian, he was an early, respectful critic of Nietzsche. At the same time, his was a luminous Christian intelligence, faithful to all the implications of the Incarnation and the spiritual nature of man. He was a deep thinker, operating effortlessly at the intersection of philosophy, theology, and political reflection.

THE THREE CONVERSATIONS

The *Short Tale* is often published alone and read alone, and this can be done quite profitably. But it is, in fact, part of the third and final conversation of Soloviev's artful and penetrating *War, Progress, and the End of History: Three Conversations*. That work is a dialogue, although not exactly a Platonic one. There is nothing aporetic about this work. We ultimately know where its author stands, since he is the philosopher Mr. Z in the conversation. Drawing liberally on Alain Besançon's lucid and penetrating book *The Falsification of the Good: Soloviev and Orwell* (1985), let me briefly introduce the background to Soloviev's *Three Conversations*.

The three conversations take place in 1899 in Cannes—more specifically, in the villa of a woman Besançon calls "an elegant, fashionable lady." This charming and genteel lady is essentially the host of the conversations. Another principal interlocutor is the General. A Russian patriot and an Orthodox Christian, the General defends nobility, common sense, and a sense of honor. He is implacably opposed to evil in its various manifestations. Unlike the denizens of the Enlightenment's moral progressivism, the General knows that evil cannot simply be wished away. He has seen evil up close, and has fought it to the death. The General knows that arms are an essential and necessary instrument for the defense of civilization and the common good.

The Politician speaks for modern Russia, for an emerging civil society in that great and troubled nation. A partisan of law, progress, and the full entrance of Russia into the civilized world, he is a liberal. But he is not a utopian, even if he places too much hope in peace and "culture" (and not enough in religion and the things of the spirit). He is a Westernizer and modernizer. Yet, despite some of his liberal illusions, he is closer to the General and the Philosopher than he is to the moralizing spiritualism of our next interlocutor, the Prince.

The Prince is, as Besançon puts it, a young man influenced "by the ideas of Tolstoy, by theosophy, and also by Russian (and other) late-19th century idealism and spiritualism." He is, first and foremost, a Tolstoyan. The Prince is a man of high principle and good character, and yet, paradoxically, as Besançon makes clear, "He also bears some similarity to Prince Myshkin [of *The Idiot*] and Alyosha Karamazov [of *The Brothers Karamazov*]. Because of this the Prince, whose good faith, impartiality and devotion to the highest moral principles are beyond doubt, appears to resemble the Prince of this world, like an icon prefiguring the Antichrist."

Besançon's arresting comparison of the moralistic Prince with the Antichrist will become clear in the course of our presentation. One of Soloviev's fundamental themes, first introduced in the Author's Preface of 1899 to *War, Progress, and the End of History*, is the idea of the "falsification of the good." Evil can ensconce itself in the very substance of the good, leading to profound spiritual, theological, moral, and political corruption, through a terrible, demonic or satanic falsification of the good. This is the most insidious path that evil can take, since it insinuates evil in the very heart of goodness. It thus poses a grave spiritual temptation for Christians and all men of good will.

TOLSTOY: PACIFISM AND MARCIONISM

As Besançon shows, the Prince is Tolstoyan, and Mr. Z the Philosopher "represents the last stage of the author's own thought." Soloviev, in this final stage of his work (1898 to 1900), rejected some of his earlier thought, or at least clarified it. But let us return to Tolstoy for a moment. As Besançon and others have pointed out, the later Tolstoy deferred to the Gospels and the Gospels alone. He wrote his own commandments in his 1881 work *The Life of Jesus: The Gospel in Brief*, which is a precursor of his much longer *The Kingdom of God Is Within You*, from a decade later. Based on a literal—and reductive—reading of "The Sermon on the Mount," Tolstoy disinterred the commandments from their larger theological and Christological contexts. Tolstoy systematically ignored all non-pacifist passages in the New Testament: He snubbed Jesus's encounter with the centurion, whom he does not tell to reject arms; disregarded *Roman* 13's endorsement of legitimate state authority; and omitted Peter's encounter with Cornelius, the Roman soldier whom he baptized in the first chapters of *Acts of the Apostles*.

As we have already noted, most orthodox readings of "The Sermon on the Mount," going back to St. Augustine's luminous commentary on that work, understand it to be a call to discipleship, not a political manifesto or program that demands a rejection of the legitimacy of armed forces within their own sphere. But this was not Tolstoy's way. He insisted on reducing Christianity to passivity, to the imperative of not resisting evil with violence and rejecting all wars. There is no place for the nation, or for patriotism, in this perversion of Christianity. His "fifth commandment" entails a comprehensive rejection of the moral and theological grounding of the nation, going so far as to say that Christian citizens should not defend their own political communities. Turning Augustine on his head, Tolstoy severs the common good from any recognition that charity sometimes demands the defense of the innocent and one's fellow citizens.

Tolstoy's Christianity calls for nothing less than the radical repudiation of the Mosaic Law. Like the early Christian heretic Marcion, Tolstoy vehemently rejects the Old Testament or the witness of the Jews as in any way pertinent for what it means to be Christian. In his view, the Christian Church and the Jewish people are permanent twin sources of corruption. Christianity, as he presents it, is not a "strictly divine revelation," but rather a moral teaching that gives "meaning to life." As Tolstoy proudly states in his preface to *The Life of Jesus: The Gospel in Brief*, in addition to finding "the pure water of life" in the scriptures, he found "an illegitimate intermixture of dirt and muck [that] had obscured its purity" as well as "foreign and ugly teachings from Church and Hebrew tradition."

In Tolstoy's hands, Christianity necessarily becomes a soft religion, an excessively "spiritualized" religion that is too confident in the inexorable victory of good over evil. Tolstoy's Christianity is willfully blind to what both the General and Mr. Z all too clearly see as the *seriousness* of evil. For them, as Besançon notes, "evil is ill-will, a hatred of God." As such, it must be fought in this world and the next with all the intensity of the spiritual warrior.

WAR AND THE SERIOUSNESS OF EVIL

The General, in Conversation One, recounts how the Bashi-Bazouks had cruelly massacred thousands of innocent Armenians with impunity. But he also describes the righteous response of the Russian Army as it, in turn, destroyed these murderous barbarians. Soloviev and the General are convinced that the righteous destruction of the murderous barbarians was a requirement of justice and true morality. The Russian Army had done the work of God. As Besançon comments, in contradistinction to Tolstoy, Mr. Z and the General are not Marcionites and in no way reject the old dispensation. They believe that Christians must fight the fight of "Joshua the warrior," which is in some part the "fight of Christ." They also believe that even God cannot force an ill-will, except by depriving it of its true source of human freedom.

For Soloviev and Mr. Z, the Prince's moral optimism derived ultimately from the Enlightenment and not from the Gospel. Like his teacher Tolstoy, he had an unfounded faith in moral progress. Tolstoy and the Prince cannot appreciate the sheer perversity of evil, its tenacious hold over the souls of men. They cannot appreciate how evil may distort or falsify goodness itself. As the *Short Tale* later makes clear, this is a terrible, but always present spiritual temptation, the temptation that evil may lodge itself even in the highest moral principles and in the kind of moral idealism represented by the Prince.

Unlike Miłosz, Besançon highlights some of Soloviev's differences with Dostoevsky. Dostoevsky was wrong in thinking that evil could be understood, as it is for so many of his characters in his important novels, as a "preliminary education" for goodness itself. For Besançon, Dostoevsky was too complacent about evil: wrongheadedly, he hated bourgeois indifference more than genuine evildoing. There is in Dostoevsky's thought a romantic attitude toward evil, which inevitably contributes to the falsification of the good. Besançon's is undoubtedly a provocative critique, but one with a large element of truth.

To sum up: We can say that for Soloviev, evil is a deadly threat to the integrity of creation and of every human soul. As such, it must be fought on the political and eschatological plains. Secular humanitarianism, with its roots in the Enlightenment, necessarily occludes the seriousness of the stakes in this great and enduring conflict between good and evil.

Let us turn again to the author's Preface to *Three Conversations*, a particularly important discussion inasmuch as it addresses Soloviev's attitude to war in general in the time before the final consummation. We have already stressed that Soloviev was not a pacifist. He believed that war was a necessary instrument for the exercise of charity and the protection of the common good. At the same time, he was no chauvinist, adamantly rejecting debased nationalism. He wanted as much peace and comity between nations, especially Christian nations, as was possible. For example, he argues that Christian nations should reconcile and promote the "closest friendship and peaceful cooperation" possible among Christian nations and states. A thoughtful reader might ask, "Why not non-Christian nations and states, too?" The answer is not too hard to discern. Soloviev believed that Christian nations had achieved a level of communion and solidarity, of civilization, of moral principle, of public and private recognition of conscience, which made genuine reconciliation among Christian states possible, and in no way utopian. Nonetheless, there were discernible limits to Soloviev's "universalism." The unity of the human race could only be achieved, he believed, at the end of time, at the moment of the final consummation.

SOLOVIEV'S INTENTION

Soloviev provides a crucial account of his aim in writing the *Short Tale* in his preface. He states that he aims to expose what he calls "the world-unifying power of the Antichrist." The Antichrist "will speak loud and with high-sounding words" that promote a moralistic falsification or corruption of the Gospel. In Soloviev's beautiful and suggestive words, he will "cast a glittering veil of good and truth over the mystery of utter lawlessness in the time of its final revelation." The *Short Tale* accordingly deals with what Soloviev unhesitatingly calls "the great betrayal." Soloviev wants to reveal beforehand this "deceptive visor under which is concealed the evil abyss"; this is his "highest aim" in writing this book. Much of the work's reflection on the Antichrist deals with the question of the relation between good and evil, and on the insidious capacity of evil to bore into the good, to turn it toward its own purposes. "All that glitters is not gold," Soloviev states near the end of the *Conversations*. We need nothing less than a philosophical theology to perceive these fundamental truths that were already foretold in scripture, particularly in those suggestive, enigmatic, and arresting pages of the *Book of Revelation*.

AN EVIL PEACE AND A GOOD WAR?

Let us turn now to the First Conversation of the three conversations on *War, Progress, and the End of History*. Along with the *Short Tale*, this is the most important moment in the work as a whole. I want to examine a particularly dramatic exchange between the Prince and Mr. Z, which has to do with the Tolstoyan Prince's claim "that war and militarism are *absolute* and *utter* evils of which humanity must rid itself at *any cost* and *immediately*." He puts out a radical challenge to Mr. Z: "Do you doubt," he asks, "that the complete and immediate suppression of this barbarism would result in any case in a triumph for reason and good?" Z takes up the challenge, responding in an equally pointed manner, "I am positively certain of quite *the opposite*." The Prince is a bit flabbergasted and inquires, "So what are you convinced of?" And Mr. Z says unflinchingly that he is convinced of the fact that war is not an absolute evil, that peace is not an absolute good, or, putting it in a simpler way, that it is "possible to have (as we do have sometimes) such a thing as *a good war*, and that it is also possible to have (as we do have sometimes) an *evil peace*."

Of course, Mr. Z would be perfectly happy to reverse that order and say, as all good Christians would, that we sometimes have bad wars, and we sometimes have good peace. But his words are shaped by the fact that he is responding to the moralistic pacifism and humanitarianism of the Tolstoyan Prince. This exchange goes right to the heart of the matter. Soloviev's Mr. Z is part of a long line of Christian reflection, from St. Paul to Augustine to Reinhold Niebuhr and C. S. Lewis, that makes a crucial distinction between murder and killing, that argues that charity, realism, and concern for conscience entail the ability and the willingness of legitimately constituted state authorities to defend their people against imminent threats to the common good.

WAR AND THE "SINGLE MURDER"

Later in the First Conversation, the chasm or divide between Mr. Z and the Prince deepens. The Prince insists, contrary to the tradition, in drawing an absolute identification between what he calls "the single murder and war" (notice that killing is assimilated to murder). He asks whether it is legitimate for a father to protect his little daughter who has come under brutal assault. Mr. Z thinks this is a misleading example. This, he says, is a matter "of natural, moral feeling." Any good father would kill the villain on the spot. "We need to examine the question in the light of a higher moral idea." So Mr. Z suggests, "Let us not take for an example a father, but a childless moralist who, before his very eyes, sees some strange and unfamiliar but feeble being, being fiercely assaulted by a cowardly villain." This "fiendish beast" is torturing his victim. Mr. Z argues that the moral impulse calls for stopping that beast by force, "however great the possibility, or even probability, of killing him may appear." In words that get to the heart of the difference between Soloviev and Tolstoy, the Prince and Mr. Z, Mr. Z says that the proper response does not entail "high-sounding phrases" or foolish refusals to distinguish killing from murder. The childless moralist who refused to come to the defense of the innocent victim would find, Mr. Z tells us, "no rest from his conscience" and would feel ashamed of himself to the "verge of repulsion." Unlike Tolstoy, Mr. Z refuses to sever Christianity from prudence, common sense, the moral law, natural conscience, or a sense that charity sometimes demands confronting evil forthrightly and unapologetically. He believes there is absolutely no convincing or compelling philosophical or theological case for allowing innocents to be butchered.

FREE WILL AND THE "BENIGNITY" OF CHRIST

Mr. Z and the Prince go on to debate the question of the absolute persuasiveness or "benignity" of the good. Following Tolstoy, the Prince believes that goodness has the power to overcome evil, just as Jesus overcame and converted the good thief, whom he told on the cross he would be with him that very day in Paradise. But Mr. Z's response exposes the superficial moral optimism underlying the Prince's position. He asks plainly why Christ could not use the power of the Christian spirit, of his own benignity, to such effect as to awaken the good hidden in the soul of Judas or King Herod or the priests of the Sanhedrin, and the evil thief, whom "everyone forgets" when the good comrade is usually mentioned?

Mr. Z adds, "Look, there is no insuperable difficulty here for positive Christian thought." But there is a profound difficulty for the Prince and Tolstoy. Mr. Z insists that the Prince will have to choose between the very "facts" of the New Testament or the "moral optimism" of the Enlightenment. He cannot continue his habit of quoting Christ and the Bible as the "highest authority," even as he holds onto an untenable and unchristian moral optimism. Mr. Z exposes the Prince's exaggerated belief in the power of Christ's "benignity." There is something unbiblical and unchristian about this secular moral optimism. It refuses to take evil seriously and it crucially abstracts from the sempiternal drama of good and evil in the human soul. For Soloviev, God scrupulously respects the free will of human beings. He cannot force evildoers to turn toward the Good or accept the grace of God.

THE GOSPEL AND "HEARTLESS LITERALISM"

Let us briefly return to a reflection of Soloviev's from the end of his life, an essay he wrote on the Spanish-American War of 1898 called "Retribution (On the Spanish-American War)." This piece can help us better understand the stakes in the confrontation between the Prince and Mr. Z in Conversation One of *War, Progress, and the End of History.*

Soloviev is an eloquent and forceful defender of the morality of military self-defense—going so far as to say that when the Spanish of the middle ages defended the Christian West against Islam, "They did not retreat from the spirit of Christ in this and their military exploits were Christian exploits." This, to be sure, is a troubling affirmation to a contemporary Christian ear tinged by pacifism and humanitarianism. But it reflects the considered judgment, the wider consensus, of the Christian tradition. Writing about the Spanish, Soloviev says there was nothing Christian about the persecution of Jews or the forced conversions of Muslims and Jews after the reconquest of Spain. He even raises the question whether their disastrous defeat in 1898 at the hands of the Americans may have involved an element of divine retribution.

Soloviev reiterates his position that the New Testament's commands on issues of the common good, charity, and the use of force should not be interpreted through the lenses of pacifism. We must always take our bearings from Christian conscience and the prudence that flows from it; sentimentality, then, is never enough. Soloviev shows that Christians can use weapons of war even if it seemingly violates the letter of the Gospel. Soloviev believes, like much of the tradition, that we need to distinguish between murder and killing. He believes that this distinction is central to both the Bible and common sense. In this essay, he relates how Metropolitan Saint Alexis, the Russian Church leader, guided by Christian conscience, rode to the Golden Horde, the Mongols, to "mollify the Tartars," and suggested to the Russian princes that they submit to the Khan as a "legal sovereign." Alexis did this not because he was a pacifist, but because he was trying to save what could be saved of the Russian state, the Russian nation, and the Christian character of the Russian people. Yet, a few decades later, the great Saint Sergius of Radonezh blessed Dmitri of Moscow in his "open-armed rebellion" against the very same Horde. He even sent two of his strongest, most athletic monks to fight with him. Soloviev adds that these two actions appear to be in "outward contrast."

Yet both Saint Alexis and Saint Sergius acted "in the spirit of Christ, for the good of the people." Soloviev adds that the action of Sergius was in "apparent contradiction to the letter of several Gospel texts." But he further notes that this was in obvious agreement with the "spirit of Christ." Soloviev adds that anyone in 1380 who would have counseled Dmitri Donskoy, Dmitri of Moscow, to lay down arms and give Russia over to destruction by the brutal Mongol Horde would not have been a Christian guided by prudence and conscience, but "a heartless scribe and literalist." Soloviev sees no ultimate contradiction between Christian piety and the requirements of true political prudence informed by the spirit of the Gospels.

For Soloviev, a Christian is always obliged to love his enemies. Unlike some Christians today who seem to believe that we have no enemies, Soloviev keenly knew that we are also sometimes obliged to fight our enemies. He believed in both chivalry and the possibility of "just war." He believed in always acknowledging the humanity of the enemy and praying for the salvation of his soul. Some scholars have asked whether Soloviev's framework of moral and political analysis is still relevant in an age of modern warfare, even nuclear warfare. I would respond by suggesting that the structure of human action and human obligations has in no essential way changed. As Raymond Aron, a foreign policy "realist" and a self-proclaimed moralist of prudence, once put it, with modern weaponry in a nuclear age, history has certainly "slowed down," but it has not fundamentally changed. The arts of conscience and the arts of prudence remain as important and as relevant as ever before. As Soloviev might say, "just war" remains a moral and political necessity in the time before the final consummation.

Let us now turn our attention to the *Short Tale*. I will provide a close reading of, and critical commentary on, this revealing text. My goal is to allow Soloviev to speak for himself and in the process to "unpack" the rich theoretical and practical resonances of the *Short Tale*. The best "method" for doing so is the time-honored practice of *explication de texte*. My summary of the text, in both its broad scope and its most revealing details, is at the service of revealing precisely what is entailed in the "humanitarian" subversion of Christianity.

The *Short Tale* is read aloud by Mr. Z. It is said to have been found in the papers of the monk, Father Pansophius, who entrusts Z with the manuscript. Father Pansophius shares both Mr. Z's and Soloviev's deepest concerns and intuitions. Arresting, imaginative, and remarkably realistic, the work remains faithful to the Bible's account of the "end times." It is also alert to the deepest and most subversive currents of religious, political, national, and ideological life in the twentieth and twenty-first centuries. As a close examination of it demonstrates, it is a genuine piece of theological-political reflection.

PAN-MONGOLISM AND THE SUBJUGATION OF EUROPE

The story is set in the twenty-first century, although it also deals with events that unfolded in the twentieth century. The first part of the work discusses the rise of pan-Mongolism. Pan-Mongolism arose in a modernizing Japan deeply suspicious of the West. The Japanese conquered China and convinced the Chinese, their hereditary enemy, that they were in fact common enemies against the Western imperialists. Together, they united to conquer Europe, beginning with Russia. Soloviev suggests that the Japanese were good at imitating the worst features of the West, taking a not-so-subtle dig at pan-Slavism, at pan-Hellenism, at pan-Islamism, at pan-Germanism, at the various national currents that surrendered to imperialism and confused legitimate national self-affirmation with conquest and imperial delusions. It should be noted that Soloviev shared the fear of a resurgent "East" that was quite typical at the time.

After years of "barbarian" subjugation, of cruel Asiatic despotism imposed on the peoples of Europe, the liberation of Europe occurs. There is a great rebellion planned by secret societies that leads to the expulsion of the new Mongols from Europe and the establishment of the United States of Europe. Initially, Soloviev points out that this United States of Europe is a union of democratic and free states. But that will change, as we will soon see.

Hard-core scientific materialists, proponents of scientism, were increasingly rare in Europe at the beginning of the twenty-first century. Soloviev reveals that there were few overt believers or "spiritualists" left in Europe. Believers constituted a remnant of a once-Christian civilization, but he adds that these believers were "thinking people." In a beautiful phrase, he remarks, they thus fulfilled "the apostles' commandment: 'Be children at heart, but not in mind.'" This might be said to be the paradox of the Christian soul: we are obliged to cultivate humility before Our Father and friend, the Creator God, but also to cultivate a certain toughness of mind and soul before the world, an ability to think like adults, to exercise the full arts of human intelligence.

THE SUPERMAN AND THE ENCOUNTER
AT THE PRECIPICE

Soon Soloviev introduces the Superman, a young man in his early 30s, who is a believer and spiritualist. He is fully cognizant of his immense spiritual gifts and has faith in what Soloviev calls the "good, God, and the Messiah." But he is also marked by an immensely destructive pride. In a particularly striking line, Father Pansophius's manuscript reads, "Eternity's all-Seeing Eye knew that this man would worship the power of evil if it ever undertook to buy him."

Soloviev here has several striking paragraphs in which he reveals the inner torment of this Superman afflicted by pride. The Superman believes in Christ, and yet distrusts him. He sees himself as the true Son of God and wonders whether in fact Christ was merely a precursor of himself, if not an outright fraud. At one point, he expresses his jealousy of Christ and yells that He did not rise. It is at this moment that we come to the incident at the precipice. The Superman denies that Christ had risen. He screams that Christ is rotting in his tomb, and with those blasphemous words the Superman is driven to despair. He goes to a precipice and attempts to commit suicide. Here, we see what can only be described as a satanic intervention. "Something buoyant, like a water spout, held him up in the air; he felt a convulsion like that from an electric shock and some force threw him back onto the cliff. He lost consciousness for an instant; when he revived, he found himself kneeling a few paces from the precipice." There he sees a figure shining with a "misty, phosphorescent glow, with two eyes that pierced his soul with an unbearably sharp light." The evil spirit speaks to him in a "hollowed and muffled voice…distinct, metallic, and completely soulless, as if coming from a phonogram." This is an arresting and perfectly believable portrait of Satan and of satanic possession. This eerie voice says to the Superman that he is the beloved son of Satan, that he should not worship the other one, the "bad one," with his son, the "crucified beggar," that God had asked for something he will not ask of the Superman, namely, total obedience and death on the cross. Satan then announces that after begetting the Superman in *beauty*, he will now beget him in *power*. The perverse imitation of scripture, of the love of the Father for the Son, is now complete.

THE OPEN PATH TO PEACE AND PROSPERITY:
A PHILANTHROPIC PROJECT

After the incident at the precipice, the Superman is filled with an immense energy and vitality. In a matter of days, he writes with "supernatural rapidity and ease" his famous study *The Open Path to Universal Peace and Prosperity*. This book literally reverses the work of Christ and voluntarily succumbs to the temptations of Christ in the desert. One is reminded once again of Matthew 4, where Christ rebukes Satan by saying, "Man shall not live by bread alone," and where the Devil took him up to a mountain and showed him all the "kingdoms of the world" in a moment of time and offered Christ all the power in the world. This is *the* powerful allure of the Antichrist's book. Willing to succumb to the temptations of Christ in the desert, the Superman offers a universal, humanitarian utopia, the Kingdom of God, or rather, the Kingdom of Satan on Earth. He will convince men that they essentially live by bread alone (or as we shall learn later, by bread and circuses). Possessed by the power of Satan, this man embodies the falsification of the good. Yet he is praised by nearly all, including most Christians. Few see the Antichrist's message for what it really is, a satanic falsification of the good.

Soloviev soon points out something of profound importance. Many Christians begin to notice that Christ is never mentioned in the pages of *The Open Path*. But most dismiss this, saying that religious writers in the past hadn't been sufficiently discreet. They had made too many references to God and had been too zealous in promoting the faith. A truly Christian spirit, we often hear, demands "active love and all-embracing goodwill." For far too many Christians, Soloviev suggests, what truly seems to matter is a humanitarianism that vigilantly makes no mention of Christ at all.

As events unfold, the once-democratic United States of Europe is transformed into an empire at a constituent assembly of the Union of European States, which takes place in Berlin. Europeans had succeeded in escaping the Mongol yoke, and a powerful brotherhood of Freemasons works assiduously for the establishment of a common executive power that will establish a true European empire. The Superman, the Antichrist, is nearly universally acclaimed as "the man who has come." He is proclaimed president for life of the European United States. This man of "youthful, superhuman beauty and power" expounds his universal program with "inspired eloquence," and "in an explosion of enthusiasm," Soloviev tells us, the "captivated and charmed assembly resolved without voting to bestow upon the Superman the supreme title of Roman Emperor." His imperium is, at this point, beyond dispute.

In tracing these events, Soloviev remains faithful to the *Book of Revelation*. We are told of the unsavory origins of the Superman. His mother is said to be a prostitute. He, like the Roman emperors, promises a "universal peace" to put an end to war. Above all, Soloviev presents the Antichrist as a humanitarian benefactor and "philanthropist." Tellingly, he is also a vegetarian and a "philozoist," somebody who loves all forms of life, especially animals. Among his achievements, he instituted among humankind "the most fundamental equality, *the equality of freedom from hunger*." This occurred in the second year of his reign. The socioeconomic problem was "solved conclusively," Soloviev writes. However, "Man does not live by bread alone." As Soloviev writes, "But if to be fed is the most important thing for hungry people, then people who have been fed want something else as well. Even animals, after eating, usually want not only to sleep, but also to play. Even more so is this true for humankind, which post-*panem* (after bread) always demands *circenses* (circuses)."

In Soloviev's account of the Antichrist, circuses replace the Word of God. It is precisely the Grand Inquisitor in Dostoevsky's *The Brothers Karamazov* who teaches that bread can substitute for the Word of God, which bread necessarily comes before virtue. In the *Short Tale*, bread is supplemented not by the Word of the Living God, but literally by magic and circuses, which substitute for the true light of the divine spirit. At this crucial point in the narrative, we are introduced to the strange magician Apollonius.

APOLLONIUS AND A NEW DARKNESS

Apollonius is described as a semi-European and semi-Asiatic figure who effortlessly united science and Eastern mysticism. Able to create fire out of the sky through combining the methods of Eastern magic and modern science, he claims to be some kind of Christian. But Pope Peter, whom we will speak about in just a moment, sees him for precisely what he is, an "indubitable deceiver." The Emperor makes this magician Apollonius a cardinal, which is very disconcerting to the genuine believers in the Christian community. The Emperor wants to preempt these concerns. People are again turning to the New Testament passages about the Antichrist, and they are beginning to speculate that this unholy alliance of magic and faith, of Church and State, is reminiscent of the Antichrist foretold in scriptures. The Emperor calls for an ecumenical council in Jerusalem, the new imperial capital, and attempts to placate Christian concerns through a series of spiritual bribes offered to each of the Christian communities. For Catholics, the Emperor offers a restoration of the papacy to Rome (it had been exiled to St. Petersburg). He offers renewed attentiveness to sacred tradition and to sacred archeology for the Orthodox and a promise of free investigation of scripture to the German Evangelicals. His seemingly generous gifts are at the service of a great deception.

The Antichrist is also a scripture scholar with an honorary degree from Tubingen. He knows scripture like Satan knows scripture in the New Testament. Pope Benedict, in the first volume of his magisterial *Jesus of Nazareth*, makes much of Soloviev's point that the Antichrist is a biblical scholar. The pope's intention is not to condemn biblical scholarship, but to remind us that, devoid of faith and confidence in the promises of God, scripture scholarship risks becoming a subversive instrument that undermines the integrity of the faith.

THE ECUMENICAL COUNCIL

At the Ecumenical Council, the vast majority of Christians—Catholic, Orthodox, and Evangelical Protestant—succumb to the charms of the Antichrist. They believe that he is a holy man and a great political bene-factor. But there are three men who stand out for their theological and moral integrity and their lucidity about the true nature of the Antichrist. To begin with, Pope Peter II, who heads the Catholic contingent to the Ecumenical Council, is a man of "peasant stock" and a preacher in the Carmelite Order. He "had been prominent in the struggle against a satanic sect that were flourishing in Petersburg and its environs" that seduced not only the Orthodox but also Catholics. He mistrusts—and is ill-disposed to—the Universal Leader, especially after Apollonius is made a cardinal and a bishop. Peter considers Apollonius to be both "a dubious Catholic and an indubitable deceiver." The pope's name obviously evokes the "Petrine" claims of the Roman Catholic Church.

Elder John, the unofficial leader of the Orthodox, is a very old man and a retired bishop. There are many conflicting legends about his alleged antiquity. Some even identify him with John, "the beloved disciple." This ancient and vigorous man has a yellowish and even greenish white hair and beard. There is an "extreme kindness" in his face. He wears a white vestment and cloak and speaks with the firmness of a faithful Christian.

The third great Christian leader at the Ecumenical Council is the leader of the German Evangelicals, Professor Ernst Pauli. He is a man of immense learning, a short man with a "wizened face," an "enormous forehead," and a "sharp nose." He is dressed in "formal solemnity," in a white tie and long pastoral dress coats with certain honorary insignias. His mannerisms are eccentric, but he, too, is forthright in his commitment to the integrity of the faith. His name obviously invokes Saint Paul, the great missionary to the gentiles.

THE ANTICHRIST REVEALED

The vast majority of Christians go onto the stage in the palace in Jerusalem to recognize the authority and primacy of the Antichrist, who has not yet fully revealed himself. The Emperor is angered by the refusal of the circles around Pope Peter, Elder John, and Professor Pauli to fully accept his spiritual and political authority. He indignantly says to the Christians, "What more can I do for you? Strange people!" Elder John replies that they will accept benefaction from him, but only if he "confesses" the name of the Lord Jesus Christ. Losing all self-control, the Emperor goes into a kind of internal meltdown, exhibiting the facial and spiritual contortions of a demonic character. He desperately tries to control himself because he knows he is revealing himself too soon.

This display is soon followed by a dramatic moment in which Elder John watches the great magician in his "enormous tri-colored cloak," covering his cardinal's purple, conducting evil manipulations beneath it while a black cloud gathers above the temple. Elder John stares "with amazed and frightened eyes" at the face of the silent Emperor, and "suddenly he recoiled in horror, and turning around, shouted in a voice, stifled with torment, 'My children, this is the Antichrist.'" At that very moment, a "deafening thunderclap, an enormous bolt of circular lightening," explodes in the temple, enveloping the Elder. The Antichrist and his insidious magician, Cardinal Apollonius, have murdered and martyred the great Elder John, who now lies dead on the floor.

Soloviev conveys this riveting, dramatic moment with the utmost realism. He perfectly portrays Elder John's moment of recognition of the Antichrist. He warns the children of Christ that evil, satanic evil, is now before them in the flesh. We witness Apollonius's evil magic, which is at the service of death and the undermining of Christ and the truth. We have one great martyr before us, and we are about to have two. The Antichrist now stands exposed for all to see.

It is precisely at this moment that Pope Peter II arises. His loud and distinct voice roars through the temple, "Contradicitur!" The pope arises, with a "crimson face" and shaking wrath and words that ring out with clarifying truth: "Our only Lord is Jesus Christ, the Son of the living God. As for who you are—you have heard. Get thee hence, Cain, brother-murderer! Get thee hence, devil's vessel! By the power of Christ, I, servant of the servants of God, expel you, filthy dog, forever from God's home and proffer you to your father, Satan! Anathema, anathema, anathema!" Pope Peter's great *contradicitur* is a moment of profound spiritual insight. We witness liberating and righteous anger in the service of Christ and truth. Pope Peter reveals himself to be a true spiritual warrior, like the archangel Michael fighting the dragon in *Revelation*. He, too, is immediately struck dead by the evil magician.

Professor Pauli now takes the lead. This eccentric (but holy) man is inspirited. Fortified by God's grace, he is filled with a new determination to safeguard the children of God. He leads the remnants of the faithful into the wilderness outside of Jerusalem to wait for the second coming of Our Lord Jesus Christ. At the same time, Apollonius is named pope, inaugurating a truly evil union of Church and State. In due time, the bodies of Pope Peter and Elder John are rescued by the faithful, each amazed to see that no deterioration has set in. The two great spiritual leaders of the Christian Church are miraculously resurrected, and in a moving and poignant scene, the churches are reunited in the hills of Jericho, with both Elder John and Professor Pauli recognizing the primacy of Peter (Soloviev, a faithful Orthodox Christian, was always an advocate of the unity of the churches under the leadership of Rome). "You are Peter," they proclaim, with evident fraternal affection and deep spiritual solemnity.

THE REVOLT OF THE JEWS
AND THE FINAL CONSUMMATION

All of this is a harbinger of the revolt of the Jews. They had been deceived by the Antichrist and had been falsely convinced that he was the Messiah, even though he was *not even circumcised*. The tale ends with a titanic cosmic battle right out of the *Book of Revelation*. The Antichrist is subdued by a massive volcano (Apollonius's magic is powerless to save him) and Christ the King comes in the clouds, inaugurating a new eschatological age for Christians and Jews alike. The Christians and Jews that were martyred by the Antichrist are here restored to life. One thing is clear: the sovereign power of God has overcome once and for all the great deceiver and his terrible minions.

THE PRINCE'S DEPARTURE

At the end of Father Pansophius's narrative, the other interlocutors notice that the Prince has gotten up and left during the crucial moment in the narrative when Elder John exposed the Antichrist. There is great significance to this, since the Prince cannot accommodate or fathom this profound eschatological battle between good and evil. His categories simply don't allow for it. Despite (or because of) his moralizing principles, he is too close to the Antichrist for comfort. He confuses love of enemies with pacifism, faith in God with moral optimism. He is a Marcionite, rejecting God's covenant with the Jews that is so central to the Christian understanding of the economy of salvation. He has no place for the spiritual warrior in God's plan—the Joshua, the Michael, or, for that matter, Christ the King, who comes again in glory and judgment at the end of time.

A DECEPTIVE MERCY

There is one other feature of the *Short Tale* worthy of reflection. The Antichrist is said to forgive all "sins past, present, and future." He is the great benefactor, demanding no punishment, no justice, and thus no repentance. He represents indiscriminate mercy that is at odds with true moral responsibility and accountability. As a matter of principle, this man, possessed by Satan, cannot take evil seriously. The Antichrist says reassuringly that "Christ brought a sword; I will bring peace. He threatened the earth with a terrible last judgment, but I will be the last judge, and my judgment will not only be a judgment of justice but also a judgment of mercy." Once again, we witness the allure that is the falsification of the good. Justice is divorced from mercy, mercy from repentance, and the goodness of God from His justice. The order of things is sundered when the mercy and justice of God are artificially divorced, a sundering of great contemporary import.

On page 37 of the Jakim translation, we observe a massive celebration by the forces of the Antichrist, after the perverse union of Church and State in the persons of the Antichrist and Apollonius is announced. Candles and rockets burst into the air, "and before reaching the ground they were turned into countless multicolored sheets of paper, with total and unconditional indulgences for all sins past, present, and future. The rejoicing of the people transcended all bounds. True, some asserted they had seen with their own eyes how the indulgences changed into disgusting toads and snakes." As Soloviev makes clear, the Antichrist's real benefaction is nothing less than a demonic emanation from Hell.

The essentially demonic character of Apollonius's magic stands revealed. But what lessons are to be drawn from this? This demonic refusal of moral responsibility, this rejection of the diptych that is mercy and justice, feeds into modern relativism. It reinforces the perverse refusal of our contemporaries to acknowledge sin, to confront our fallen human natures that are so desperately in need of the friendship and grace of God.

In *The Falsification of the Good*, Alain Besançon perceptively remarks that Soloviev's touchstone was always Christ. Soloviev thought it was necessary to get the Incarnation right, and in doing so, to reject the insidious temptation of Marcionism. We need to affirm what the Jews brought to the economy of salvation, the Covenant, as well as circumcision, the mark of the Covenant. The Antichrist's refusal to be circumcised turns out to be reason for the great Jewish Revolt that ultimately brings him down. In sharp contrast, in the final culmination, Christ comes on the clouds as a crucified king. He, not the mendacious Antichrist, embodies the true satisfaction and fulfillment of the Jews' long-held messianic expectations.

THE THREE ORTHODOXIES

Returning to the principal interlocutors in the *Three Conversations*, we must note that the General stands for the defense of the people, for saving lives, and thus, paradoxically, for war as an instrument, not of inhumanity, but of the common good. The Politician rightly stands for civil peace, stability, law, and order. Z stands for the union of the Christian faith with political reason. There are genuine truths in all of these perspectives and affirmations. Besançon insightfully remarks that "It seems that to Soloviev, the three orthodoxies would stand or fall together, and that the clear vision of one allowed a glimpse of the others. On the last page of this account, everything is restored to its rightful place and mankind rejoices together in the true conception of the good, now that the falsifier has been banished."

The cooperation of the three great orthodoxies against the falsification of the good is the deepest of Soloviev's lessons. But what is the relevance of this parable today? To begin with, we, the living, we who remain faithful to the promises of God, must not succumb to the temptations in the desert. We must not confuse the promises of God with the kingdom of heaven on Earth. The Gospel in no way promises us an earthly paradise, far from it. It in no way promises an eradication of evil through goodwill or humanitarian wishful thinking—or even through the sheer power of Christ's "benignity." We must not confuse the witness of faith with fuzzy sentimentality, naïveté toward evil, and a "philanthropy" that is untethered from the truth of Christ.

In contradistinction to Tolstoy, Soloviev believed nations still have a central role to play in the Christian dispensation. Christians must not forget the great commission where Jesus says to His Apostles, "Go forth to all the nations and baptize in the name of the Father, the Son, and the Holy Spirit." The Christian God is both transcendent *and* incarnate. He promises something much more precious than bread and circuses, or even social justice, which in its quasi-socialist forms is inseparable from an excessive passion for equality, and even an encouragement of envy. We must not confuse sincere love of the poor, an undeniably great injunction of the Gospel, with a humanitarian or socialist political project to bring about heaven on Earth. That is the dangerous path pursued by Dostoevsky's Grand Inquisitor, who remains so far from the authentic spirit of the Gospel.

THE HUMANITARIAN FALSIFICATION OF THE GOOD

Christians, of course, are called to exercise political reason and Christian charity at the service of improving and reforming the world. But as Soloviev teaches, we always ignore the power of evil at our own peril. Christianity has nothing to do with unlimited faith in progress, or a false and naïve confidence in moral optimism. We too must fight the battles of Joshua and Michael, and not merely on the eschatological plain. With Mr. Z, we must affirm that there sometimes can be a *good war* and an *evil peace*. Peace is not coextensive with pacifism for the ancients, for the Jews, or, for that matter, in the Christian tradition. Christianity must stand guard today, refusing to confuse itself with utopianism, sentimentality, humanitarianism, and a pacifism that ignores common sense (so precious to Soloviev) and distorts Christian conscience. True Christianity affirms the truth of pagan nature, the Jewish Covenant, and political reason and political civilization. All are allies in the common struggle against ideology or the demonic falsification of the good.

Soloviev's parable is all the more relevant in a world that increasingly conflates Christianity with secular humanitarianism and is blind to the chasm that separates them. Sadly, this blindness has increasingly affected the Church in Rome itself. As we have noted, the present pontiff, no Antichrist to be sure, is half-humanitarian. But the same cannot be said of his great predecessor, Pope Benedict, who never ceased repeating with Soloviev that the Christian religion is not reducible to a humanitarian moral and political message. Soloviev and Benedict are great—and much needed—witnesses to what is at stake in the humanitarian subversion of Christianity that has for a long time now haunted the modern world.

Soloviev speaks above all to faithful Christians, but his writings have lessons for all men of good will. As R. R. Reno has recently written in *First Things*, "one need not adopt Soloviev's apocalyptic imagination (or his Christian faith) to recognize a truth his fantasy brings forward." The spirit of authentic human unity must respect the shared loves and goods that belong to particular peoples who reflect an essential part of the divine plan. Humanitarianism subverts human dignity when it identifies our highest aspirations with a peace and prosperity, a godless philanthropy, shorn of any concern for that which transcends humanity and which ultimately grounds our dignity as spiritual beings. And believers and non-believers alike can learn from Soloviev how to take evil seriously again and avoid a moral optimism that blinds us to the sempiternal struggle between good and evil in the human soul.

• SOURCES AND SUGGESTED READINGS •

I have drawn on Soloviev's *Lectures on Godmanhood*, with an introduction by Peter Peter Zouboff (Semantron Press, 2007). See p. 18 of Zouboff's introduction for an illuminating discussion of how Soloviev came to see that "the kingdom of heaven cannot be fully actualized in the conditions of this material world."

My reflection on Soloviev is profoundly indebted to Alain Besançon, *The Falsification of the Good: Soloviev and Orwell*, translated by Matthew Screech (London: Claridge Press, 1994). This work, a masterpiece of political-theological reflection, originally appeared in French in 1985. For Besançon's introduction to the principal interlocutors in the "three conversations," see pp. 13–21. For a very helpful discussion of Tolstoy and Tolstoyism, including his Marcionism, see p. 25. On the "seriousness of evil," see p. 51. On the Antichrist as a "religious impostor," see pp. 57–62. For a particularly revealing discussion of how the three "orthodoxies" ultimately stand or fall together, see p. 76.

For Czesław Miłosz's Introduction, see Solovyov, *War, Progress, and the End of History: Three Conversations*, translated from the Russian by Alexander Bakshy, revised by Thomas R. Beyer, Jr. (Lindisfarne Press, 1990), pp. 7–13. See p. 12 for the citation. I have drawn extensively from the Author's Preface, pp. 24–25. For the discussion of murder and war in Conversation One, see in particular pp. 39–44. For the limits of Christ's "beginity" to transform souls, see p. 63. For the Prince's departure from the conversation and the ultimate significance of *A Short Tale of the Antichrist*, see pp. 193–194.

I have also relied on Boris Jakim's wonderfully clear and expressive translation of *A Short Tale of the Antichrist* in Vladimir Solovyov, *Sophia, God & A Short Tale of the Antichrist, also including At the Dawn of Mist-Shrouded Youth* (Semantron Press, 2014), pp. 5–41. For the discussion of pan-Mongolism, see pp. 5–6. For the "contradictions" in the Antichrist's soul, including his demonic pride, see pp. 11–12. For the dramatic incident at the precipice, see pp. 14–15. On *The Open Path to Universal Peace and Prosperity*, see p. 15. On philanthropy and the Antichrist's humanitarian political program, see p. 20. For the initial discussion of Apollonius, see p. 21. On the moral and religious integrity of Pope Peter, Elder John, and Professor Ernst Pauli, see pp. 25–26. On the exposure of the emperor as the Antichrist foretold in scripture, see pp. 32–33. On the false mercy of the Antichrist, see p. 13 and especially p. 37. On the union of the churches under Pope Peter, see pp. 38–39. On the final consummation and the defeat of the Antichrist, see pp. 40–41.

For Tolstoy's general view of Christianity and his hostility to both the Church and the Old Testament, see the Preface to his *The Life of Jesus: The Gospel in Brief*, a new translation by Dustin Condren (New York: Harper Perennial, 2011), pp. xxi–xxii. For Tolstoy's new commandments and his aversion to the nation and national self-defense, see pp. 35–36 and p. 109.

Soloviev's 1895 essay "Nationality from a Moral Point of View" can be found in *Politics, Law, and Morality: Essays by V. S. Soloviev*, edited and translated by Vladimir Wozniuk, Foreword by Gary Saul Morson (Yale University Press, 2000), pp. 37–53. I have drawn extensively on pp. 112–113 of Soloviev's 1898 essay "Retribution (On the Spanish-American War)" in the same volume.

CHAPTER FOUR

The Humanitarian Ethos

As this whole book confirms, if secular modernity has a religion, it is undoubtedly "the religion of humanity" (for the moment, I will leave to the side the immensely destructive totalitarian political or secular religions of the twentieth century). The idea of a secularized Christianity, of a Christianity without Christ or transcendence, was first theorized by Saint-Simon and Comte in the nineteenth century. These self-described "positivists" were astute enough to realize that humanity could not live well without religion, even if it was still necessary to dispense with a transcendent God and a moral law that appealed to something beyond the immanent needs of human beings. Formalizing what Aurel Kolnai called "a non-religious, immanentistic, secular moral orientation," Saint-Simon and Comte saw this as a quasi-religious replacement of *authentic* religion. (Kolnai made clear that authentic religion always entailed a "corporate" and "socially relevant... outlook which contains a reference to a 'higher' Power.")

As the Hungarian-born moral and political philosopher Kolnai (1900–73) noted in his remarkably penetrating and prescient 1944 article "The Humanitarian versus the Religious Attitude" (the article appears as an Appendix to this book), humanitarianism is "the standard type of non-religious philosophy" that has arisen "on a soil tilled by Christianity." Christianity is "universalistic, personalistic, and moralistic" and thus readily gives rise to a humanitarian distortion of itself. Those who lose confidence in the promises of God, or repudiate the supernatural dimensions of their faith, fall back on a humanitarian ethos where "man as such" is the "measure of everything." They tend to reduce Christianity to a concern for "social welfare" and the alleviation of poverty and suffering. Humanitarianism eventually is seen as that part of Christianity that is truly "essential" and "worthy of respect." This view is held not only by secular humanitarians but by many liberal or demi-Christians who identify Christianity exclusively with a project of this-worldly amelioration.

Kolnai insists that humanitarianism takes its bearings from an "immanent," and remarkably truncated, view of human beings—it does not acknowledge the hierarchy of goods and values that characterize the moral order and the life of the soul. It combines relativism and moralism (each equally insistent) in a way that is characteristic of a "morality" that loses sight of the capacious natural and supernatural destinies of human beings. Humanitarianism also gave rise to totalitarian secular religions, such as Communism and National Socialism, that abhorred soft humanitarianism and aimed to build the "kingdom of heaven on earth." With Communism in mind, Reinhold Niebuhr spoke suggestively of the differences between "hard" and "soft" utopians and liberal humanitarianism's vulnerability to co-optation by those who will do anything to build a "new man" and a "new society."

Much more emphatically than democratic humanitarianism, totalitarian secular religions repudiate the moral law and are radically anthropocentric in character. They posit a collective self-deification of man that Kolnai insists always leads to man's self-enslavement (see his magisterial 1949 essay "Privilege and Liberty" for a particularly profound development of this theme). As the great Russian writer Aleksandr Solzhenitsyn argued in his 1978 Harvard Address, the more moderate versions of humanitarianism and anthropocentricity are always vulnerable to appropriation by more radical and consistent versions of atheism, materialism, and humanitarianism. Liberal and democratic versions of humanitarianism are then haunted by a totalitarianism that culminates in what Kolnai calls "the 'identitarian' loss of liberty and personality." Drawing on Kolnai and Solzhenitsyn, one can understand "the self-idolatry of society"—society and humanity worshiping itself and succumbing to a totalitarian order—as *one* possible outcome of the humanitarian reduction of man and reality to a merely material order.

Kolnai insisted that more moderate and decent forms of humanitarianism are dialectically dependent "on the dwindling resources of Christianity." Writing in 1944, he acknowledged that the "modern civilization of Western mankind" was not wholly irreligious; it was "still in part actually Christian." That is surely less the case today. But already, he saw that the religious attitude and ethos was rapidly giving way to an immanentistic humanitarian ethos that no longer knew how to look up to everything in the order of things that was truly substantial and truly noble. And he drew this philosophical conclusion: the flattening of souls and perspectives that accompany humanitarianism badly damaged "moral cognition" as such.

To be sure, as a philosopher, a Christian, and a phenomenologist of the moral life, Kolnai appreciated that the cultivation of moral virtue and the recognition of the distinction between Good and Evil did not depend only on religious faith. A cursory examination of the world shows that unbelievers can be just and kind and can exercise self-control. Catholicism itself posits "the immanent distinction of Good and Evil"—of an objective moral order available to man as man. But Kolnai convincingly argues that the differences between the religious attitude and the humanitarian one are not merely a matter of a different motivation for moral behavior. To be sure, the humanitarian is able to discern the "moral sense" as a guide to understanding the nature and needs of human beings. Yet humanitarianism ultimately impairs moral cognition, since a horizon that deifies undifferentiated "human needs" has a hard time acknowledging the "unpleasant," the truly morally demanding dimensions of the moral life. The moral life, in the full sense of the term, demands internal struggle and a willingness to come to terms with "the equally unpleasant consciousness of moral guilt or inferiority." The conscience makes moral demands on human beings who are sensitive to its requirements. Repentance and the *metanoia* of souls (the heights of the moral and spiritual life from a Christian point of view) have little place in a moral horizon shaped by exclusively humanitarian concerns. Kolnai makes his point quite emphatically: "humanitarian and religious morality must *always* be different in *quality*."

Moral cognition is deepened and enriched by a truly substantial account of the moral life and the human soul. Without a religious appreciation of the full range of human needs (and not the cacophony of human wants posited by humanitarian materialism), the spiritual dimensions of human life are all but forgotten. Additionally, religion in general, and

Christianity in particular, has a unique capacity to reconcile "personal freedom, dignity, selfhood and vitality with social discipline and coordination." Like his great nineteenth-century liberal conservative forebear Alexis de Tocqueville, Kolnai cannot imagine the safeguarding of the mores of society without the survival of a vigorous and demanding religious sensibility. Religion helps to make human beings and societies "whole," to reconcile the sacred and the mundane, the freedom of persons and the requirements of civilized order. Without religion, and in the West that means biblical religion, the person becomes a mere individual and society loses the capacity for a common good and the kind of collective action that respects the moral integrity of human beings. The Christian notion of the person affirms human liberty and dignity while avoiding the illusion of thoroughgoing human "autonomy." The dignity of man ultimately depends upon the primacy of the Good and the affirmation of the sovereignty of God (which, contra voluntarism, has nothing to do with divine willfulness), a point well understood by Orestes Brownson.

Kolnai is particularly sensitive to the self-destructive dimensions of the humanitarian ethos. A society imbued with a religious sensibility holds human beings responsible for their actions and knows how to punish wrongdoing, even as it is open to the redemption of souls through supernatural grace. Under humanitarianism, there is a hesitancy to punish since the very notion of evildoing—of a fundamental moral scissure in the human soul—is rejected in the name of the alleged social origins of evil and criminality. Paradoxically, the same soft morality readily hardens when it is a matter of the "unfit for life"—writing in 1944, Kolnai already foresaw how the humanitarian ethos would effortlessly combine opposition to capital punishment with fevered support for abortion and euthanasia. A discerning reader of Kolnai cannot help but ask how much of contemporary Christian opposition to the death penalty, for example, is rooted in attitudes and assumptions that owe more to secular humanitarianism than the full weight of the Gospel and Christian tradition. In a late modern and hyper-democratic political order (one paradoxically ruled by increasingly unaccountable technocratic elites imbued with "humanitarian" sensibilities), religion is relentlessly "democratized" and increasingly fails to appreciate the myriad differences between itself and the humanitarian attitude and ethos. Writing in the midst of the Second World War, Kolnai believed that this was a distinction that Catholics could still self-consciously teach to the world. In the first part of the twenty-first century, this is the very same distinction that a Catholic thinker such as Kolnai can teach a Church that is increasingly tempted "to kneel before the world," in Jacques Maritain's suggestive formulation. For increasingly today, the Church is tempted to interpret the truth of the faith in light of humanitarian concerns and considerations mixed with an increasingly thin and fraying patina of Christian categories, language, and assumptions.

The last major Catholic figure to fully appreciate this distinction, to make it a fundamental theme of his thought and his pontificate, was Pope Benedict XVI. As we have seen, in his 2007 Regensburg Address he emphatically insisted that Christianity was in no way reducible to a "humanitarian moral message." The pope emeritus saw the conflation of Christianity and humanitarianism as the source of great evils, a threat to the integrity of the Gospel, the moral law, and the Christian faith. As he makes clear in his preface to the revised edition of *Introduction to Christianity*, Benedict has little regard for the ethos of "May '68," defined as it was by an assault on traditional authority, a loosening of moral bonds, and a simultaneous indulgence toward Communist totalitarianism, particularly of the Castroite and Maoist variety.

It will be useful to recapitulate some of our argument from Chapter One. In Chapter Two of the first volume of *Jesus of Nazareth* ("The Temptations of Jesus"), Benedict expertly explains how the accounts of the temptation of Jesus in the desert in the Synoptic Gospels sketch a critique of humanitarianism *avant la lettre* (Dostoevsky already had this intuition, as powerfully evidenced by "The Grand Inquisitor"). As Benedict shows in that chapter, those who put bread and power above the word of God, the moral law, and the spiritual needs of humanity ironically cannot produce the bread needed by human beings to live. They end up tyrannizing the bodies and souls of human beings. This is a vital lesson that Benedict draws from the terrible experience of humanity with Marxism in the twentieth century. Building on the insights of Vladimir Soloviev, Benedict suggests that the Antichrist will come to sight as a humanitarian thoroughly committed to a "planned and thoroughly organized world, where God may have his place as a private concern but must not interfere in our essential purposes." Benedict notes that Soloviev presents the Antichrist as a man who worships "well-being and rational planning," the author of a seductive tract called *The Open Way to Universal Peace and Prosperity*. Benedict also notes the fundamental antithesis between Barabbas, the armed revolutionary who desires a messianic kingdom on Earth, and the essentially trans-political message and mission of Jesus Christ. Benedict's Jesus of Nazareth is in no way a secular humanitarian. Quite the contrary, he is secular humanitarianism's most lucid critic. His insights are perfectly congruent with Brownson's, Soloviev's, and Kolnai's.

Let us return to Kolnai. In important respects, he anticipated Benedict's concerns and arguments. He saw that humanitarianism had a "fatal tendency towards materialism," stressing the "material needs" of human beings at the expense of their souls. He argued that in a "climate of irreligion," or of religion distorted by humanitarianism, man's "spiritual functions and capacities" would "inevitably be understimulated, undernourished, underexercised, and be condemned to atrophy." An inordinate emphasis on man's "sovereignty" would paradoxically degrade man, "displace his center of gravity into the nether regions of his being," and undermine authentic humanism and moral decency.

Kolnai stands out as one of the most compelling and persuasive critics of human self-sovereignty (although a relatively neglected one) among the important thinkers of the twentieth century. He was a true philosopher and moral phenomenologist, one whose "unprejudiced contemplation of 'humanity'" drew him toward religion and the Christian faith. Moral phenomenology came first, followed by conversion to the Catholic faith in 1926. And as he points out in his Political Memoirs (finished in 1955 but only published posthumously in 1999), G. K. Chesterton (and to a lesser extent Husserl) was the bridge for Kolnai between these two worlds. Such a disinterested reflection on the "greatness and misery of man" leads one to appreciate man's "fallenness" (marked by the never-ending drama of good and evil in the human soul) as well as his unique "ontological nobility." By recognizing the limits inherent in the human condition, one paradoxically comes to see the dignity of every created human being in a cosmic order that is not indifferent to the human good. Dignity and nobility point beyond themselves to the source of all nobility—the justice, grandeur, and goodness of God. A true openness to mundane reality allows one to see that human beings exist "in relation to a super-human reality," one that ultimately grounds human freedom, dignity, and responsibility. An authentically philosophical reflection on the nature and needs of the human being reveals "the radical inadequacy" of every form of humanitarianism. Human needs must be understood capaciously, in light of the fullness of Reality.

One of the remarkable things about "The Humanitarian versus the Religious Attitude" is that in it Kolnai grasped the logic of democratic humanitarianism—its essential features and telos—long before it began to display its full nature. The same can be said of other authors we have highlighted. The piece is thus as prescient and discerning an analysis of our present situation as one can read and confront today. Much like Tocqueville's remarkably discerning analysis of the democratic soul in volume 2 of *Democracy in America*, Kolnai's dissection of the humanitarian attitude and ethos is even more compelling—more true—than it was at the time of its original publication. Like Tocqueville's account, it holds up a mirror to our democratic souls and reveals what is missing when we jettison an account of human destiny that does justice to the fullness of the human person and the richness of the moral life.

Kolnai does not hesitate to argue that humanitarianism ultimately entails the "moral abandonment" of man—a profound diminishment of our humanity. He saw, for example, that a reductive emphasis on "human needs" would soon abandon anything requiring a demanding and humanizing sexual morality. An emphasis on self-restraint, not to mention moral purity, would come to be seen as "delusive, neurotic, wayward" and thus in need of a thorough "rationalization" and "dissolution." Kolnai foresaw that the Catholic positions on divorce, contraceptives, and abortion would become unintelligible to those who have succumbed to a humanitarian ethos (and would even be seen as "revolting and scandalous" rather than "too lofty and rigorous"). And a misplaced emphasis on human sovereignty, on man's "empire over himself," would lead to an indulgence toward suicide and mercy killing. All of this has come to pass. As Kolnai strikingly puts it, humanitarianism may not encourage out-and-out iniquity, but it soon abandons ethical criteria necessary for a life well lived and a genuine political common good.

Kolnai was also sensitive to the ways that humanitarianism's inordinate emphasis on "the present moment" would affect the integrity of individual and collective life. Irreligious humanitarianism does not appreciate the elements of "eternity" in the temporal realm; one lives for the "present moment" and increasingly deemphasizes "the preservation and the status" of one's family. Societies imbued with a humanitarian attitude would soon have problems reproducing themselves and maintaining a healthy level of "biological continuity." One need only look at the demographics of late modernity in contemporary Europe to see how prescient Kolnai was. The French tellingly speak of *dénatalité*—the "unbirthing" of France.

A religious attitude, in contrast, allows one to fully appreciate the links between our forebears, ourselves, and those who are yet to be born. It allows for a full appreciation of the continuity of civilization. And as the great French Catholic poet and philosopher Charles Péguy affirmed with wonderful clarity, the Christian proposition invites a constant reflection on the intersection of the temporal and the eternal. Christianity in no way entails a repudiation of the natural or temporal realm, even if it "relativizes" our "natural egoism."

In fact, by severing our ties with transcendent reality, humanitarianism tends to undermine man's sense of reality and sheer capacity to enjoy temporal reality. Kolnai suspected that an undermining of the capacity of human beings to look beyond the sovereign self diminished the human spirit and man's ultimate ability to enjoy life. In his view, the Puritans of old paradoxically had more "gusto and vigor" than those who were obsessed with self-preservation and the petty and paltry pleasures with which late modern man occupies himself. Human beings have a "need" for a "meaning of life" that transcends a reductive account of human needs—a need that is not without support in the order of things. To affirm what is truly substantial and noble in human life, man must cease to "set himself at war with Being." He must repudiate the project to "emancipate" himself from an order of things that makes demands on our freedom. The rejection of irreligious humanitarianism is the vital precondition for the recovery of an authentic humanism and of a Christianity that does not bow before the idols of modernity.

• SOURCES AND SUGGESTED READINGS •

"The Humanitarian versus the Religious Attitude" originally appeared in *The Thomist* in 1944 and was republished in Kolnai, *Politics, Values, and National Socialism*, an excellent edition of Kolnai's essays on moral, political, and phenomenological themes written between 1925 and 1970. It is republished at the end of this volume. The volume was edited by Graham McAleer and published by Transaction Publishers in 2013. Readers interested in the themes of this essay should pursue the full range of Kolnai's reflection on Christianity and politics in *Privilege and Liberty and Other Essays in Political Philosophy*, edited by Daniel J. Mahoney (Lexington Books, 1999). The title essay, from 1949, is of particular pertinence. It is a rich reflection on the "totalitarian" and "identitarian" subversion of human liberty. It is written from an expressly Catholic point of view.

Kolnai's posthumously published *The Utopian Mind and Other Papers*, edited by Francis Dunlop (Athlone, 1995) is also relevant to the topic. Humanitarianism and utopianism share a denial of intrinsic evil and the moral scissure in the souls of human beings. The recognition of the inability of "value" and "reality" to wholly cohere is a precondition of the moral life and of decent and free (non-utopian) politics.

Pope Benedict's critique of humanitarianism is most fully articulated in Chapter Two ("The Temptations of Jesus") of volume I of *Jesus of Nazareth* (New York: Doubleday, 2007), pp. 25–45. See pp. 31–33 for a discussion of Marxism, and pp. 40–41 for discussions of Barabbas and Soloviev and the Antichrist.

CHAPTER FIVE

Solzhenitsyn's *Red Wheel*: A Tough-Minded and Humane Christian Vision

It is not uncommon for readers of Aleksandr Solzhenitsyn's final novel, *The Red Wheel*, to draw comparisons with another Russian masterpiece, Leo Tolstoy's *War and Peace*. Like its predecessor, *The Red Wheel* is a massive, sweeping work, 6,000 pages divided into four "knots"—"Narratives in Discrete Periods of Time"—and incorporating actual historical events that changed the course of Russian history, and of human civilization, too. It commences as a historical novel, but in sections it turns into dramatic history with no fictional characters at all, only historical ones. Both epics delve into the deepest moral and religious concerns, and the status of the two authors as moral authorities in their own times adds to the parallel.

But for all their similarities, *The Red Wheel* is, in fact, a firmly anti-Tolstoyan work (one will find suggestive affinities between Solzhenitsyn's and Soloviev's respective critiques of Tolstoy). Indeed, Tolstoy's vision of human affairs is a direct target of Solzhenitsyn, and much of the speech and action of *The Red Wheel* explicitly renounces it. To put it bluntly, Tolstoy's famous ethic of Christian love fails miserably in Solzhenitsyn's universe. In his pacifist, rationalist understanding of Christ's teaching, Tolstoy forgets that every human being and citizen has moral and political responsibilities, and that to ignore them, especially in the face of evil, is not a commitment to a higher summons. It is a betrayal of man and God.

The critique runs throughout *August 1914*, the first knot of *The Red Wheel*, and the early chapters of *November 1916*. *August 1914* begins with Sanya Lazhenitsyn's visit to Tolstoy to discuss some of the writer's core ideas. Sanya (a character based on Solzhenitsyn's own father) travels to Yasnaya Polyana, Tolstoy's estate, with the hope of initiating a conversation with the renowned sage. They engage in a brief, if one-sided, conversation. Sanya suggests that the great writer exaggerates the power of love, ignores the limits of universal benevolence, and mistakenly identifies what is good and reasonable. In a word, he charges that Tolstoy underestimates the power of evil, that he fails to acknowledge original sin. For Sanya, evil can never be understood as mere ignorance. As he puts it, "evil refuses to know the truth, rends it with fangs." Tolstoy believes that universal benevolence is the path to an unprecedented society of peace and brotherhood. But Sanya, though timid, has become a renegade Tolstoyan who can no longer abide the master's system and the illusions about the human heart that accompany it. He is instead attracted to the ideas of *Vekhi* (*Landmarks* or *Signposts*), the great intellectual manifesto published in 1909 by a group of independent Christian pluralist thinkers (Berdyaev, Struve, Bulgakov, and Frank, among others). These figures challenged the Russian intellectual class, decried the cult of revolution, defended political moderation, and, above all, argued for the priority of the things of the spirit over material goods. Reading *Vekhi* "pierced [Sanya] to the quick," Solzhenitsyn writes. As the opening pages in *August 1914* make clear, Sanya is searching for a settled point of view, and Tolstoy no longer provides satisfying answers.

This is not the last we hear of Tolstoy. Later in *August 1914*, after Sanya and his student friend Kotya have volunteered for the armed forces, they encounter the philosopher Varsonofiev, the so-called stargazer, who is impressed that these young men think of themselves as patriots even though patriotism is no virtue in "progressive" intellectual circles. During their conversation, Sanya tells a revealing story about a literate Russian peasant who had written to Tolstoy. The peasant had suggested that the Russian state was like "an overturned cart," broken and hard to move, and he asked how long working people would have to go on dragging it. "Wasn't it time to get it back on its wheels?" Tolstoy's answer is uninspiringly fatalistic. He says that if the cart is righted, those who turn it over will only jump inside and make ordinary Russians pull it once again, leaving them no better off than before. What, then, were they to do? "Let the wretched cart look after itself!" Tolstoy exclaims. "Just ignore it altogether! Unharness yourselves and go each his own way, in freedom. Then your lives will be easier."

This answer is wholly inadequate for Sanya and for us. Tolstoy's disdain for Russia amounts to disdain for the common good. As Sanya puts it, "This refusal to help everyone else haul the cart was what first turned me against Tolstoy. His hazy oversimplification." Here is Tolstoy's counsel in all its practical import: Do nothing but withdraw. The term *passivism*, coined by scholar Vladislav Krasnov in a 1986 essay in *Slavic Review*, neatly unites the pacifism and passivity of Tolstoy's ethic. It is forthrightly counterproductive and cautious. Another character in *The Red Wheel*, the neo-Tolstoyan General Blagoveshchensky, reveals a personal rule derived from it: "One must never take any abrupt and decisive steps of one's own." The irony is obvious: What kind of outlook is that in a commander of armed forces?

The opposite of passivism is found in Georgi Vorotyntsev, a colonel in the Russian army and the fictional protagonist of the work. One critic terms him "the direct bearer of Solzhenitsyn's distress." Vorotyntsev belonged to a circle in the military that was known as the "military Renaissance," "a small, tightly knit group [that] had come together in the General Staff Academy, consisting of soldiers with a feel for twentieth-century warfare" who understood the importance of new knowledge and approaches and knew that modernity posed existential challenges that Russia had to face. Solzhenitsyn says they are "soldiers who realized that Peter the Great's banners and Suvorov's fame would do nothing to strengthen or protect Russia, that the need was for modern technology, modern organization, and fast and furious thinking."

Vorotyntsev's urge to act climaxes in a late scene in *August 1914* in which he confronts time-servers at military headquarters. General Samsonov, the Russian commander who committed suicide during the Battle of Tannenberg, possessed faith, piety, and love of country but suffered, too, from the debilitating passivity of the old Russia. Now, as others falsely blame him for all the mistakes of a Russia that had mobilized too quickly, Vorotyntsev rises before Grand Duke Nikolai Nikolaevich, the commander in chief of the tsarist forces, and defends Samsonov's honor. "But the main reason for the destruction of Samsonov's force is that neither it nor the Russian army as a whole was ready to take the offensive so soon," he alleges. The mobilization of Russia's forces had not been nearly complete; the country needed two full months to mobilize, and it sent men disastrously unprepared into action after only two weeks. This guaranteed disaster at the Battle of Tannenberg. The others grow angry, especially when Vorotyntsev identifies a different cause of failure: the desperate efforts on the part of military and political officials to satisfy Russia's French ally at all costs.

Yet Vorotyntsev is not a wholly unproblematic figure. In *November 1916*, a personal affair both undermines his marriage and distracts him from rallying the forces of good against the coming disaster of the revolution. In the final, dramatic scene of *April 1917*, however, he recovers and helps organize a conference of officers, even as Russia's military and political authorities decline into fatal ineffectiveness. It is Vorotyntsev who helps initiate what will become the White Movement. We know from other writings of Solzhenitsyn's, such as the play *Prisoners*, that Vorotyntsev will end up as a White officer and continue resisting the Soviet state for a good 20 years. Vorotyntsev is a man made for action—the opposite of the generals, who, under the influence of Tolstoy, succumb to an enervating fatalism.

The great political and nonfictional protagonist of *The Red Wheel*, at least of *August 1914* and *November 1916*, is Pyotr Stolypin, prime minister of Russia from 1906 to 1911. Solzhenitsyn places almost all his hopes for the survival of a decent, free, and tradition-minded Russia on the shoulders of this great statesman, who would die at the hand of an assassin in September 1911 at the age of 49. It is he who arduously pursues a "middle line of social development" by taking on the armed revolutionary left, solidifying a constitutional order in Russia, and guaranteeing hardworking peasants the right to own their own land by leaving the centuries-old reparational commune, where land was held and worked in common.

Much of the lengthy Chapter 65 of *August 1914* lays out the Russian statesman's "principal idea" that the reparational commune was finished. Stolypin's idea was one of "shining simplicity—yet too complicated to be grasped or accepted." He knew the faults and limits of the commune and reached a pointed conclusion: "The reparational commune reduced the fertility of the land, took from nature what it did not return, and denied the peasant both freedom and prosperity." Rejecting all romanticism about the commune, he concluded: "The peasant's allotment must become his permanent property." If Russia could create a new class of peasant, citizen-proprietors, Stolypin reasoned, some of the challenges of modernity would be met and overcome. These men would have a stake in the system, be loyal to the monarchy, and help "defeat revolution through reform."

In this passage, Solzhenitsyn does inquire, however, whether the self-denial (or the harmonization of the will of the individual with that of the commune) required by the old system leads to "something more valuable than harvests and material well-being." Perhaps there is more to life than the development of private property. Perhaps there is something to be said for a system of paternalistic constraints that cramp the freedom of the individual but reflect "the people's philosophy of life, its faith." In a crucial passage at the beginning of Chapter 65 of *August 1914*, Solzhenitsyn nicely recapitulates, without in any way endorsing, the moral teaching of the Slavophiles, who find the spiritual greatness of the peasant in his "eternal subordination, an awareness of oneself as an insignificant particle." But as Solzhenitsyn makes clear, Stolypin has excellent reasons for rejecting this position. Thinking that way about the *mir*, or commune,

> makes action impossible. Stolypin was always a realist. With him, thought and action were one. No one can ask the people to behave like angels. We have to live with property, as we live with all the temptations of this life. And in any case, the commune created a good deal of discord among the peasants.

The commune, in the guise of creating an angelic community, in fact created endless discord, and the novel shows it. It fostered oppression, enervated the will, and got in the way of creating a decent, hardworking, self-respecting political and economic community.

Stolypin's idea is to take a bet on the strong and determined rather than on the idle and the drunk. As he lies dying in his bed after being shot at the Kiev Opera House in September 1911, he reflects on his achievement of liberating the hardest-working peasants from the tyranny of the commune. He is convinced that he "defeated revolution with reform" by bringing a strong, orderly, self-confident constitutionalism to bear in Russia. But he also appreciates the arduous and fragile character of his own middle path between revolution and reaction, and he is desperate to get an indifferent tsar to reflect more seriously on these matters.

It is important to understand how Solzhenitsyn's political, spiritual, religious, and philosophical convictions are played out in these events and expounded by the characters. At one point, a dialogue between Sanya Lazhenitsyn and Father Severyan, a 35-year-old army chaplain, extends through two full chapters of *November 1916*. Severyan is a dark-haired, bearded Russian Orthodox cleric, the crème de la crème of the priesthood. A man of good character, great intelligence, and lucid articulateness, he is also a Christian who is not taken in by facile progressivism or the humanitarian distortion of or substitution for Christianity that is now the rage among a certain kind of intellectual. He is the perfect interlocutor for Sanya.

Their dialogue on a rainy night on the front goes right to the heart of Solzhenitsyn's deepest concerns. The first part treats the Old Believers, a splinter group that refused to conform to liturgical changes. Sanya thinks that they were unjustly persecuted for remaining true to the faith of their fathers. He also suggests that they were the most energetic, diligent, morally discerning, and religiously serious of Russians. In this passage, Sanya uses the same kind of language to describe the persecution of the Old Believers in the seventeenth and eighteenth centuries that Solzhenitsyn uses in other works to describe the persecution and killing of kulaks, religious believers, and other "enemies of the people" in Leninist-Stalinist Russia in the 1920s through the 1950s. In other words, he sees the struggle against the Old Believers as an effort to destroy the flower of the Russian nation.

This important discussion of the Old Believers and their place in historic Russia is quickly followed up by a lengthy discussion of Tolstoy. Once again, Sanya insists that Tolstoy is too sweeping in his critique of the faith of old Russia. He is particularly struck by Tolstoy's hatred of the cross and all it represents. Tolstoy, he tells us, advises his listeners not to regard representations of the cross as sacred, "not to bow down to it, not to put it on graves, not to wear it." "Such insensitivity! I can't go along with that," he cries. "You know the saying—a grave uncensed is just a black hole. And it's even truer of a grave without a cross. No cross? When there's no cross, I get no feeling of Christianity."

This dramatic intervention by Sanya leads to a crucial moment in the dialogue when Father Severyan raises the all-important question of whether Tolstoy was a Christian at all. This question understandably shocks Sanya. His jaw drops, and he asks, "Not at all?" Father Severyan answers that Tolstoy made a raid on the Gospels for his own purposes. He appealed to "political passions" and encouraged a hatred of both church and state. His readership was impressed less by his appeal to religion than by his frontal assault on the political and religious establishment. Moreover, the Father says, Tolstoy's teaching is "useless" for society—no society could exist on its basis. Besides, the liberal public did not care about his spiritual quest. "It had no use for religion reformed or unreformed."

This sustained indictment is followed by a penetrating discussion of war and pacifism. Everything in Tolstoy (his hostility to Orthodox Christianity, his fatalism, and his pacifism) originates in the injunction to "Resist ye not evil"—that is, in his hyper-literal interpretation of the Sermon on the Mount. This is crucial for Sanya. The young officer is still influenced by Tolstoyan pacifism. He is fighting on the front, but with a guilty conscience. He remains a quasi-pacifist or at least a guilty warrior. Father Severyan suggests to him that the true faith understands his ambivalence and reminds him that ancient Christian warriors who returned from a campaign were not immediately absolved. They were made to do penance first. He also suggests to Sanya that there is another way out of his dilemma: "Change your ideas." It is time to cease being quasi-pacifist, and to disengage Tolstoyan pacifism from the core of Christian wisdom.

Father Severyan does not consider war to be the worst of evils. It is one evil among others tied up with the fallen nature of man. "At no time has the world been without war," he states. "Not in seven or ten or twenty thousand years. Neither the wisest of leaders, nor the noblest of kings, nor yet the Church—none of them has been able to stop it." Hotheaded socialists won't end it, nor will rational and just wars be sorted out from the rest. Father Severyan's enunciation is precise: "War is the price we pay for living in a state. Before you can abolish war you will have to abolish all states. But that is unthinkable until the propensity to violence and evil is rooted out of human beings. The state was created to protect us from violence." In a memorable passage, Father Severyan lists five human evils worse than war:

> An unjust trial, for instance, that scalds the outraged heart, is viler. Or murder for gain, when the solitary murderer fully understands the implications of what he means to do and all that the victim will suffer at the moment of the crime. Or the ordeal at the hands of a torturer. When you can neither cry out nor fight back nor attempt to defend yourself. Or treachery on the part of someone you trusted. Or mistreatment of widows or orphans. All these things are spiritually dirtier and more terrible than war.

The "real dilemma," Father Severyan concludes, "is the choice between peace and evil." War may be an evil, but it is only a special case of evil "concentrated in time and space." Whoever rejects war must also reject the state. But to reject the state is to forget the universal evil instilled in men's hearts. You are not going to overcome the evil of worldliness with antiwar demonstrations, by processions along the streets with signs bearing slogans. Those like Sanya who joined the fighting army are not to be condemned— "they naturally went where so many others were suffering." Those who can be "rightly reproached" are those who do not "struggle against evil."

Sanya listens and begins to turn away from pacifist doubts and the false view that Tolstoy represents a true, primitive, or authentic Christianity. Evil must be resisted, and war paradoxically forms part of that resistance. This is not to give uncritical support for World War I—far from it. Solzhenitsyn saw the war as an unmitigated disaster for Russia, a crucial moment in that monumentally destructive negation of civilized order, which was "the red wheel." In his 1983 Templeton Lecture, Solzhenitsyn freely spoke of the First World War as a calamity for Russia and the whole of Europe, a calamity that reflected a loss of a "divine dimension" to human consciousness on the part of a Christian civilization that was losing its spiritual moorings and its sense of sacred limits and restraint. Solzhenitsyn is confident that if Stolypin had lived, he would have kept Russia out of the war, or at a minimum would have been a voice for sanity in the weeks and months leading up to it.

Why, then, is Solzhenitsyn so hard on the pacifistic distortion of Christianity? Because evil is real, rooted in fallen human nature, and must be resisted if the things of the soul are to be preserved. The state is a powerful instrument for keeping evil at bay and for safeguarding the foundations of civilized order. One must resist the facile negation of the common good, which is so typical of Tolstoy. The spirit of pacifism also dulls one to the malign efforts of those revolutionary nihilists such as the Bolsheviks, committed as they were to the destruction of Christian civilization. Against Tolstoy, Solzhenitsyn urges what he once called "the active struggle against evil," which entails the maintenance of an imperfect order against ideological demons who are animated only by the spirit of pure revolutionary negation.

The focus of *The Red Wheel* turns out not to be Red October, as originally planned when Solzhenitsyn designed 20 knots that would go all the way up to 1922 (with five epilogues going up to 1945). In *March 1917* and *April 1917*, the focus becomes the February Revolution, the ostensibly "democratic" revolution that unseated tsarism. Here was the true revolution and the enduring disaster. Solzhenitsyn came to see the October Revolution as a secondary coup d'état made possible by the ineffectual character of the new order that had arisen after the overthrow of the tsarist regime in February 1917.

With *March 1917* we arrive at the "revolution at last" (the discrepancy in months is due to the fact that Russia still adhered to the Julian calendar). This novel is also the work of faithful historical reconstruction and contains many chapters of "dramatized history." These finely drawn chapters capture the sheer ineptitude of the tsarist regime, infinitely more ineffectual than repressive. As revolution unfolds, a weak and equivocating Nicholas II has no sense of what is really happening in St. Petersburg, the capital of the Russian empire. His ministers, from Prime Minister Golitsyn to Minister of Interior Protopopov, are nullities, men incapable of serious thought and action. They have ceased to govern in any meaningful sense of the term. They dither as St. Petersburg succumbs to revolution, spurred on by (false) rumors that the government is deliberately withholding bread from the people. The tsar is preoccupied, as always, with returning to his family at Tsarskoe Selo, even as revolution unfolds. Only a few rare individuals from Rittikh, the firm and intelligent Minister of Agriculture (a potential heir to Stolypin), to some brave isolated officers (like Colonel Balkashin in Chapters 101, 122, and 185) who fight to preserve an ordered liberty, show a capacity to stand up to the revolutionary delirium so powerfully conveyed by Solzhenitsyn. Solzhenitsyn uses all the powers of literary art to show a civil society blindly celebrating the collapse of civilized order (and this during war) and oblivious to the dangers that accompany the radical revolutionary transformation of a political order still capable of reform. In deftly drawn street scenes—short, dramatic chapters—Solzhenitsyn conveys the inebriation of crowds who are caught up in a playful but deadly revolutionary carnival. The playful carnival quickly turns violent—with looting, the freeing of violent criminals from prisons, and deadly assaults on policemen. Red flags appear everywhere, and hints of more radical revolution down the road are apparent from the first days of the revolutionary cataclysm. Once again, fashionable left-liberals see "no enemies to the Left," a blindness that will soon spell their doom and the doom of Russia.

The liberals and socialists in the parliament or Duma are expertly—and damningly—portrayed. The monarchist Rodzyanko, the head of the Duma, is remarkably self-absorbed and too enamored of the Duma's prerogatives to grasp the dangers of full-scale revolution. He gets carried away by events and helps form a "Provisional Committee," which almost immediately begins to lose power and prestige to the revolutionary Soviets, dominated as they are by Mensheviks and later by the even more "revolutionary" Bolsheviks. Solzhenitsyn paints a portrait of Aleksandr Kerensky as a disingenuous demagogue interested only in destroying the tsarist order and oblivious to the dangers posed by the totalitarian left. The self-promoting Kerensky applauds "revolutionary law" and delights in speechifying. He helps destroy a decent, if imperfect, political order and can ultimately build nothing constructive in its place. In Chapter 44, the conservative liberal intellectual Pyotr Struve captures both the ineptitude of a government that has "fallen asleep" and the illusions of an opposition (in the Duma and elsewhere) that doesn't realize that freedom cannot flourish without a state. "This is the flaw in our consciousness: living in our country in a permanent state of rebellion." What Russia is missing is a firm, energetic, and freedom-loving leader of the type embodied by Stolypin. As we have seen, this great conservative reformer was the scourge of the revolutionaries and the reactionaries alike. His "strength of spirit," as Rittikh nicely puts it, was sorely absent in 1917. He was a world-class statesman who grasped "the burden, grief, and joy of responsibility!", words that could have also been uttered by other great statesmen such as Winston Churchill or Charles de Gaulle. Solzhenitsyn means for us to reflect on what Stolypin's absence in 1917 meant for Russia and the world.

The old order thus needed to be preserved and reformed, built on the precious and fragile legacy of Stolypin, whose fortitude was needed instead of the tsar's inaction and pusillanimity. The entire narrative of *March 1917* conveys this point. Solzhenitsyn puts it with even more force in *Reflections on the February Revolution*, originally completed in 1983 and published in 1995 (and reprinted again in 2007 for the 90th anniversary of the February Revolution of 1917). The four parts that make up this essay were originally written to be introductions to the four parts of *March 1917*. But Solzhenitsyn decided that they would distort the literary form of the presentation, so he published them separately.

As he writes in that work, "monarchy is a strong system on the condition that the monarch is not too pusillanimous. Comport oneself as a Christian on the throne, agreed, but not to the point of forgetting one's duties or the nation's business in a way that blinds oneself to approaching catastrophe." In that same essay, Solzhenitsyn faults Tsar Nicholas for failing to take a series of defensive moves, including sending reliable troops to crush the rebellion in Petersburg, making sure bread was readily available, and cutting telegraph lines between Petersburg and Moscow. These steps might have thwarted the revolution before it had time to get off the ground. If the tsar had sent reliable troops to Petersburg, he would have risked bloodshed, but Solzhenitsyn also notes everything that would have been averted. It's a tough-minded reflection by a Christian who knows that difficult choices have to be made in this imperfect world. Even if some had died in the effort to maintain a legitimate political order, this "would not have had the least resemblance with the Civil War which lasted three years on the vast expanses of Russia, with the criminal exactions of the Chekists [the secret police], the epidemic of typhoid, successive waves of crushed peasant rebellions, the Volga basin suffocated by famine—and then a half-century of the internal gnashing of the gulag." The tsar's weakness, especially his overweening concern for his family, led to a betrayal of the Russian nation and people by a man whose responsibility had been conveyed to him by "heredity, by tradition, by God Himself." And once this decent but mediocre tsar fell, Russia was left to the equally pathetic inaction and lack of will of the "democratic" provisional government and of the liberal and socialist forces dominating the Duma.

The pathos of that outcome is dramatized most sadly in Chapter 27 of *April 1917* when disabled veterans assemble at the Duma and the Tauride Palace and implore the government to do something about Lenin and his provocateurs. Lenin has just returned to Russia with the help of the duplicitous German enemy. These disabled veterans rightly see him as a traitor actively undermining the war effort. These men of sacrifice and suffering fathom the malevolence of the Leninist left, but the provisional government is blind and feeble. No one comes to their defense. The Leninists beat up some of the disabled veterans and hurl obscenities. All the leaders of the new Russia can do is mutter pieties about free speech, a free speech that is said to belong even to those who plan to bury civilization once and for all.

What was needed was Solzhenitsyn's tough-minded Christianity. The humane Christian realism of Father Severyan in *November 1916* has no passivity or pusillanimity. It defends human agency against those who reduce human freedom, whether they be ideological thugs or idealistic pacifists. Politics is not the most important thing in the world, but politics still matters. The state matters. And it is impossible in this fallen world to imagine a decent human order that does not encourage citizens and believers alike to take seriously the full range of one's political and civic responsibilities.

I hope that this treasure that is *The Red Wheel* (Solzhenitsyn always considered it to be his most significant work) will become better known as the years go by. One positive sign is the recent republication by Farrar, Straus and Giroux of paperback editions of both *August 1914* and *November 1916* as part of an effort to commemorate the centenary of World War I. Perhaps most promisingly, the Kennan Institute has announced its support for a translation project that will make the remaining knots of *The Red Wheel* available over the next several years. The University of Notre Dame Press has committed itself to publishing the whole of *The Red Wheel* in English translation as well as *Between Two Millstones*, Solzhenitsyn's fascinating and deeply informative memoir of his 20 years in the West.

As Georges Nivat, the great Franco-Swiss Solzhenitsyn scholar and Russianist, has nicely suggested, Solzhenitsyn is the author of two great "literary cathedrals." The first is *The Gulag Archipelago*, the definitive exposé of ideological despotism. The other is *The Red Wheel*, the equally definitive account of how the demons of revolution and nihilism came to triumph in the first place. Most discerning critics appreciate the literary and moral greatness of *The Gulag Archipelago*. A careful, serious, and open engagement with *The Red Wheel* makes clear that it, too, is a literary masterpiece. It is a sprawling and fascinating mix of philosophical and moral discernment, literary inventiveness, and historical insight that sometimes strains the novelistic form, but it is also one of the great works of moral instruction of the twentieth century.

• SOURCES AND SUGGESTED READINGS •

The Red Wheel (*Krasnoe Koleso*) appeared as volumes 11 through 20 of Solzhenitsyn's *Collected Works* (*Sobranie sochinennii*, Vermont—Paris, 1983–1991). The revised and definitive version has been published by Vremya (Moscow) in the 30-volume

Collected Works. I have also consulted the excellent French translations (Paris: Fayard) which are available for all of *The Red Wheel.*

August 1914 (New York: Farrar, Straus and Giroux, 1989) and *November 1916* (New York: Farrar, Straus and Giroux, 1999) are available in superb translations by the late Harry T. Willetts. I have also consulted the new edition of *March 1917*, Book 1 (Chapters 1–170), expertly translated by Marian Schwartz, which was published by the University of Notre Dame Press in October 2017. Struve's account of the opposition's addiction to a "permanent state of rebellion" can be found on p. 203, Chapter 44 of the 2017 Notre Dame edition. See pp. 448–449 of Chapter 117 for a discussion of Stolypin's "strength of spirit," so absent in the governing class in March 1917, and for the quotation about "the 'burden, grief, and joy of responsibility!'—as Stolypin used to say." This is a beautiful and apt description of the responsible statesman's soul.

Selections of key chapters from *March 1917* and *April 1917* are also available in Edward E. Ericson, Jr., and Daniel J. Mahoney, eds., *The Solzhenitsyn Reader: New and Essential Writings, 1947–2005* (Wilmington, DE: ISI Books, 2006).

For the revealing exchange between Sanya and Tolstoy see *August 1914*, Chapter 2, pp. 12–19, especially pp. 16–18.

The discussion with Varsonofiev appears in Chapter 42 of *August 1914*, pp. 334–348. For the passage on the "overturned cart," see p. 341.

For an excellent account of Solzhenitsyn's critique of Tolstoyan fatalism and "passivism," see Vladislav Krasnov, "Wrestling with Lev Tolstoi: War, Peace and Revolution in Aleksandr Solzhenitsyn's New *Avgust Chetyrnadstatogo*," in *Slavic Review* 45 (4), Winter 1986: 707–719.

For General Blagoveshchensky's Tolstoyan fatalism and his passivity in battle, see *August 1914*, p. 417.

For Vorotyntsev and the "Military Renaissance," see *August 1914*, pp. 98–99.

See Chapter 82 (pp. 834–846) of *August 1914* for Vorotyntsev's impassioned critique of Russia's failed military strategy and the mendacity of blaming everything on Samsanov.

For the Bolshevik assault on the disabled veterans and the accompanying impotence of the liberals in the Duma, see Chapter 27 of *April 1917* in *The Solzhenitsyn Reader*, pp. 453–459. For Vorotyntsev and the beginnings of the White movement, see the final dramatic chapter (186) of *April 1917* in *The Solzhenitsyn Reader*, pp. 460–463.

Solzhenitsyn's fullest treatment of Stolypin's character, ideas, and statecraft appears in Chapter 65 of *August 1914*, pp. 529–606. The crucial passages on the limits of "the reparational commune" appear on pp. 530–531. For Stolypin's death scene, see Chapter 69 of *August 1914*, pp. 643–652.

The extremely rich dialogue between Sanya and Father Severyan occurs in Chapters 5 and 6 of *November 1916*, pp. 40–56. I have quoted extensively from these two chapters. The crucial passage on the five human evils that are worse than war appears on p. 53 of Chapter 6.

For the discussion of Nicholas's fatal flaws, I have relied on Solzhenitsyn's *Réflexions sur la révolution de Février*, translated by Nikita Struve (Paris: Fayard, 2007). I thank Stephan Solzhenitsyn for his translations from the original Russian.

See Georges Nivat, *Le phénomène Soljénitsyne* (Paris: Fayard, 2009) for an indispensable discussion of both *The Red Wheel* and *The Gulag Archipelago* as "literary cathedrals."

CHAPTER SIX

Pope Francis's Humanitarian Version of Catholic Social Teaching

We turn now to Pope Francis, a pontiff at the intersection of authentic Christianity and a misplaced contemporary humanitarianism. Pope Francis is widely acclaimed today, less for his Catholic wisdom, I would suggest, than for the fact that he is perceived by secular (and some religious) opinion as some kind of "progressive." People who have never deferred to papal authority or shown any interest in the rich tradition of Catholic social thought have endorsed his proclamations in the spirit of secular ultramontanism. Whether this will lead many to return to the Church or reconsider "the truth about man" that it proffers is highly doubtful. There is, alas, an element of the *bien-pensant* in Francis's papacy, a tendency in his utterances and self-presentation to confirm widely held left-liberal elite opinions about politics and the world. (Theodore Dalrymple is particularly good on this subject.)

The consensus around Pope Francis is selective and tends toward the ideological. His admirers, and the pope himself sometimes, confuse Christian charity with secular humanitarianism. Francis's ill-disciplined, off-the-cuff remarks are treated with utmost seriousness, and the (considerable) part of his thought that is in continuity with his great predecessors is largely ignored, if not explained away. Among conservative Catholics there is deep suspicion of the pope and a growing sense that he confuses his personal judgments, largely shaped by the Argentinian experience, with the full weight of Catholic wisdom.

How does one find one's way in the midst of this confusion? How does one separate the admirable Christian witness of Pope Francis from what resembles a secular cult of personality? I would begin by suggesting that we take Pope Francis at his word and respectfully (and frankly) engage his thoughts and assumptions in the light of the tradition of Western political philosophy and the rich trove of wisdom inherent in the Catholic social tradition. We need a "hermeneutic of continuity" that forthrightly confronts Francis's ample continuities and equally ample discontinuities with the great tradition that preceded him. We owe the pope both respect and the full exercise of the arts of intelligence.

CARING FOR OUR COMMON HOME

Pope Francis's May 2015 encyclical *Laudato Si'* (*Praise Be to You*) is a perfect illustration of these continuities and discontinuities. It has largely been received as a secular intervention in political life and one that has undoubtedly cheered the hearts of those committed to draconian measures to address climate change. This reading of the encyclical does not do justice to what is specifically Catholic about *Laudato Si'*. There is much about it that is thoroughly orthodox and even traditionalist in orientation. One does not have to be completely enamored of Saint Francis's romantic personalization of the natural world ("Brother Sun, Sister Moon") to be moved by the poetic theologizing about the created order that informs the first parts of the encyclical. Pope Francis repeats old Christian wisdom of a decidedly anti-modern cast when he laments the project of modern mastery which reduces human beings to "lords and masters" of nature. He affirms human uniqueness, a uniqueness "which transcends the spheres of physics and biology" (*LS*, section 81), even as he emphasizes our stewardship over the whole of creation. For Francis, that is the true meaning of human "dominion" and responsibility to Creation. Pope Francis enhances the very rich ecological reflections of his immediate predecessors, Saint John Paul II and Benedict XVI (see Chapter 4 of Benedict's *Caritas in Veritate* [*Charity in Truth*]), by providing the full theological grounds for a "deep communion" (*LS*, section 91) between human beings and the rest of nature. His regular reminders of human uniqueness (*LS*, section 81) prevent a drift toward pantheism or a mere romanticization of nature. However, as Father James V. Schall has noted in a commentary on the encyclical, Francis's is more a theology of creation than a theology of redemption, and is thus incomplete.

Pope Francis's theological defense of biodiversity, which takes up much of the early part of the encyclical, probably understates the fact that organisms and species come and go quite independently of the alleged rapaciousness of human beings. Perhaps this shows the limits of a "Franciscan" personalization of nature, where nature and the living things of the world become more than metaphorical "brothers" and "sisters." Such thinking encourages stasis and ignores the dynamism inherent in nature and in human societies. This brings us to one more tension in the encyclical: a society that aims to be static, that simply rejects human mastery over nature, that attempts to preserve pristine nature as it is, all in the name of not "sinning" against creation, cannot meet the goal of providing "sustained and integral development" for the poor, a goal that is so central to Francis's pontificate.

The best part of the encyclical is Part Three, on "The Human Roots of the Ecological Crisis." There, Francis reminds us that technological progress is not coextensive with moral progress. This is a theme that goes back to Rousseau and Sismondi and that was repeated with eloquence and grace by twentieth-century anti-totalitarians such as Solzhenitsyn and Havel. Francis reminds us of the central role that technology played in the murderous rampages of Communism and Nazism (*LS*, section 104). The pope draws on the insights of the conservative German Catholic theologian and philosopher Romano Guardini to the effect that an increase in power does not necessarily entail progress and cannot inform "the responsibility of choice that is inherent in freedom" (*LS*, section 105). In the best tradition of conservative moralism, he counsels "clear-minded self-restraint" and a "setting of limits." Do his progressive admirers appreciate just how traditional these themes are? Francis's critique of a one-dimensional "technological paradigm" (*LS*, section 108) that assumes that economics and technology can solve all our problems, without the help of virtue and self-limitation, is salutary and consistent with the best Catholic and conservative wisdom (here, I do not use the word "conservative" in any partisan American sense, but refer to the broader moral tradition of the West that the Church—and men of good will outside the Church—wish to conserve).

Pope Francis is not wrong when he argues that "modernity has been marked by an excessive anthropocentrism" linked to a "Promethean vision of mastery over the world" (LS, section 116). Man is not God and should eschew all projects of human self-deification. He should not confuse the progress of the human soul with limitless technological or economic progress. All social progress demands respect for limits and efforts at self-limitation. These are words of wisdom that the secular world desperately needs to hear. At the same time, the Church needs to be open to the contribution that markets and technological innovation can make in addressing a problem such as climate change. The pope almost always identifies markets with greed, inequality, economic imperialism, and environmental degradation. His judgments about capitalism are quite summary and far from equitable.

Moreover, he is completely silent about the horrendous environmental devastation that accompanied and characterized totalitarian socialist systems in the twentieth century. This is a theme that Solzhenitsyn, who can be fairly described as a conservative green, repeatedly emphasized in writings such as Letter to the Soviet Leaders (1974) and Rebuilding Russia (1990). The concentration and centralization of state power went hand in hand with a brutal exploitation of nature and a complete lack of political accountability. Democratic capitalist systems, in contrast, have remarkable powers of self-correction. As George Will has argued, one has only to compare the levels of pollution in Dickens's London with those in today's London, or look at the remarkable transformation of the Thames over the past 50 years, to question Francis's identification of capitalist "progress" with the accumulation of "debris, desolation, and filth" (LS, section 161). These are empirical judgments, and the pope has no special authority in this realm. He should avoid such invective, which stirs up passions rather than enlightens. He needs to exercise his judgment with the appropriate measure rather than assuming the truth of "doomsday scenarios" that automatically lead to "catastrophes" (LS, section 161). Occasionally, Pope Francis notes that "business is a noble vocation" that "is directed to producing wealth and improving the world" (LS, section 129). But he spends much more of his time excoriating the profit motive and lecturing his readers on the evils of air-conditioning (LS, section 55) and the full array of consumer goods. He even has a good word to say about subsistence farming, a way of life the poor are so desperate to escape that they flee to monstrously large, and dangerous, cities.

I want to say something about the place of the poor in Pope Francis's reflections. He loves the poor and reminds us of our special duty to be concerned with their fate. At his best, he is a poet and theologian of charity. He can only be admired in that regard. Still, the biblical conception of the poor is not reducible to material poverty. One only has to think about the tension between the "poor" and the "poor in spirit" in the Synoptic Gospels' accounts of the Sermon on the Mount. The poor are not always victims (Aristotle argues that they can be as rapacious and despotic as the rich), and terrible crimes were committed in the name of the poor or the "proletariat" in the twentieth century. In the summer of 2015, *The Economist* called Pope Francis a "Peronist," correcting those who see in his social reflection a softness toward Marxism, although this is sometimes apparent in his utterances, too.

The characterization is apt. But as one observer has noted, Peronist populism created a "rancid political culture in Argentina," one that emphasized class struggle and redistribution above lawful wealth creation. Argentina went from being the 14th richest country in the world in 1900 to the 63rd today. Sadly, one sees some evidence that Pope Francis is rather indulgent toward despotic regimes that speak in the name of the poor—his recent silence about the persecution of mainly Catholic dissidents in Cuba was deafening (the Cuban-born Catholic scholar Carlos Eire of Yale even wrote on the *First Things* website about a "preferential option for the oppressors"), and he was remarkably affable both with Cuba's late tyrant emeritus, Fidel Castro, and with the ever more dictatorial Evo Morales in Bolivia. During the welcoming ceremony at Jose Marti International Airport in Havana on September 19, 2015, Pope Francis spoke of his "sentiments of particular respect" for Fidel Castro, a totalitarian tyrant who subjugated the people of Cuba for 50 years and viciously persecuted the Church. Perhaps the Holy Father needs to read Armando Valladares's 1982 book *Against All Hope*, a searing account of life in Castro's gulags and political prisons. All of this is disappointing, to say the least. The poor need political liberty, too, and the opportunities that come with private property and lawfully regulated markets. Even more disturbing is the claim by an acolyte of the pope, Bishop Marcelo Sanchez of the Pontifical Academy of the Social Sciences, that "China is the best implementer of Catholic social doctrine" today (*Catholic Herald*, February 6, 2018). This blindness toward totalitarianism and indulgence toward regimes that actively persecute faithful Catholics are hallmarks of Francis's papacy. It is striking that Pope Francis rarely reiterates the Church's defense of private property, a central concern of Catholic social teaching going back to Pope Leo XIII (read the very forceful defense of private property—and trade unions—in *Rerum Novarum* [*Of New Things*], as well as that encyclical's absolute condemnation of socialism). I will put the matter bluntly: A faithful Catholic is not obliged to be a Peronist. We are obliged to live the Gospel and to exercise prudential judgment, rooted in reality and reflecting the best secular and Christian wisdom.

The pope should also be more careful about endorsing "a very solid scientific consensus" (*LS*, section 23), as he calls it, on the causes and likely results of climate change. As Father Schall has noted, "his is an opinion backed by some evidence." But "satellite readings of the planet's temperature are different from U.N. computer-generated statistics. The planet's temperature has not changed in recent decades." Climate change has always been a reality. Think of the "Little Ice Age," which brought ice and bitter cold to North America and northern Europe for centuries. Some Russian scientists believe the global warming that has existed is attributable to changes in solar spots. One should also note that a considerable "scientific consensus" existed in support of the Club of Rome's 1972 report that predicted, in dramatically apocalyptic tones, that the earth would run out of crucial resources by the year 2000. That model was also computer-generated. The "ecological conversion" (*LS*, section 216) recommended by the pope must avoid the secular apocalypticism that informs a good part of the environmental movement. As Pope Francis knows, and as the beautiful prayers that conclude his encyclical attest, we Christians worship the Triune God and not "Gaia" or Mother Earth.

Pope Francis is admirably critical of abortion and population control as means of addressing our ecological "crisis." He even criticizes "gender theory" (have you heard that reported in media accounts?). But the apocalyptic dimensions of the encyclical have won him some strange bedfellows. The Vatican invited the German scientist John Schellnhuber to Rome as one of the speakers when the encyclical was released, even though he is on record as saying that the earth can sustain only a billion people. There is a totalitarianism lurking in this German scientist's assumptions. It is not one shared by Pope Francis—far from it. But why does the Vatican associate with scientists and publicists (the pro-abortion Naomi Klein also comes to mind) who are openly committed to an anti-Catholic and anti-human agenda? This is disheartening for faithful Catholics who also oppose political extremism.

Pope Francis mentions "subsidiarity" only once in his encyclical, but he waxes poetic about a "true world political authority" (*LS*, section 175). When Pope Benedict raised the same issue in *Charity in Truth*, he cautioned against the potentially despotic effects of centralization and wrote about subsidiarity at great length. Francis does not break with his predecessor, but he shows, as *First Things* editor R. R. Reno has argued, remarkable faith in the capacity of an elite of international technocrats to govern the world. Will they be friendly to the Christian vision of the human person? Will they respect human liberty and the requirements of subsidiarity, of decentralization, and of a kind of self-government worthy of man? Shouldn't Francis's thought-provoking critique of "the technological paradigm" apply to the vision of a world state itself? These and other questions persist in an attentive reading of *Laudato Si'*.

To his credit, Francis has invited true debate and discussion from Catholics and all people of good will. Catholic social thought did not begin with this encyclical, nor will it end with it. We owe this pope our respect and our judgment, but not automatic agreement with empirically questionable premises, ones that sometimes reflect an ideological cast of mind.

THE JOY OF THE GOSPEL

Pope Francis has emphasized the joy that accompanies the proclamation of—and fidelity to—the Gospel. His 2013 apostolic exhortation *Evangelii Gaudium* (*The Joy of the Gospel*) is a call to recover the "good news" in all its amplitude. One must never lose sight of "the delightful and comforting joy of evangelizing," of spreading God's word with the love and hope that are the hallmarks of God's Kingdom.

The Joy of the Gospel is not a document devoted mainly or exclusively to the social teaching of the Church. But Chapter 4 of the exhortation ("The Social Dimension of Evangelization") touches on fundamental aspects of the Christian engagement with the contemporary world. In important respects it is a mini-encyclical or exhortation on the Church's social and political teaching. Like all such documents, it draws on the work and insights of Francis's great predecessors. But as we shall see, its appropriation of Catholic social thought is surprisingly selective. Gone are the Church's warnings against ideological utopianism (see Benedict XVI's *Spe Salvi*), its qualified defense of a market economy rooted in rule of law and sound mores (see John Paul II's *Centesimus Annus*), its defense of private property as necessary for personal dignity and the exercise of the moral virtues (a defense common to Thomas Aquinas and Leo XIII), and its forthright condemnation of the socialist confiscation of human freedom (see in particular Pius XI's 1931 encyclical *Quadragesimo Anno*). Nonetheless, Pope Francis repeatedly states that his fierce condemnations of liberal capitalism are in full continuity with the Church's social teaching. Indeed, the Church has always condemned "unfettered capitalism," although outside the limited circle of libertarian ideologues, it is hard to find anyone who believes that the market ought to be truly unfettered or treated as an end in itself. That said, what is distinctive to Francis is a series of *emphases* that tend to give a distinctly "progressivist" turn to Catholic social reflection.

Pope Francis rightly emphasizes that religion, and the Christian Gospel, cannot "be relegated to the inner sanctum of personal life, without influence on societal and national life, without concern for the soundness of civil institutions, without a right to offer an opinion on events affecting society" (*EG*, section 183). Pope Francis is no partisan of "the naked public square." But rather than identifying Christian engagement in politics with Catholic statesmen from Thomas More in the sixteenth century to Adenauer and de Gaulle in the twentieth, the pope evokes the social witness of Saint Francis of Assisi and Blessed Teresa of Calcutta. That is his right. Both great souls preach an eschatological holiness that is undoubtedly a precursor of the Kingdom. But they are not remotely statesmen and have little to say about the properly civic dimensions of the common good in a sinful and fallen world. Francis's emphasis on Christian political engagement has a decidedly perfectionist cast. In the same section of his apostolic exhortation, Francis speaks about the desire of "authentic faith" to "change the world," to "fight for justice," and to engage in the activity of "building a better world." Christians must indeed fight for justice, but as St. Augustine taught in *The City of God*, no political order is simply just, and no political order will or ever can be. That is to hope for too much in a fallen world, as the Christian thinker Thomas More reminds us. There are better and worse political regimes, but there are limits to justice inherent in the human condition. We Christians must indeed work for decency and must be fearless witnesses to truth and justice. But as the great political theorist Eric Voegelin liked to point out, in some profound sense the world cannot be "changed." Efforts to establish the kingdom of heaven on Earth lead to misery and tyranny, and place humanitarian concerns above Christian truth and the adventure of the soul. At his best, Pope Francis grudgingly acknowledges this truth. He is no advocate of inhuman utopianism. But his unqualified appeals for us to "change the world" have a tendency to "immanentize" the Gospel, to emphasize this-wordly amelioration above the supernatural destiny of man. Again, it is a question of emphasis, in this case of what the Hungarian-born moral and political philosopher Aurel Kolnai called "misplaced emphasis." Francis's language, unintentionally no doubt, reinforces the progressivism inherent in a distinctively modern or late modern sensibility regarding politics.

Pope Francis desires a "Church which is poor and for the poor" (*EG*, section 198). This affirmation is in the best tradition of Christian wisdom and moral witness. But as we have already pointed out, Francis rarely emphasizes the tension between "the poor" and the "poor in spirit" that is so central to the Gospel's account of what is today called "the preferential option for the poor." Aristotle teaches, and modern experience confirms, that the poor as a sociological category can be selfish, rapacious, and prone to manipulation by demagogues, even as the rich can be oppressive and unjust and confuse their good fortune with moral virtue. Pope Francis even refers to the "goodness" of the poor (*EG*, section 199), a statement that can give rise to misunderstandings. At the same time, the pope is careful to state that "the option for the poor is primarily a theological category rather than a cultural, sociological, political or philosophical one." The option for the poor cannot be reduced to government programs or "unruly activism" and above all suggests a "true concern for the person" (*EG*, section 199). These are welcome qualifications that, alas, do not always shape this pope's practical engagement with the world.

The Joy of the Gospel defends solidarity and subsidiarity (as all recent popes have done) and does not necessarily endorse statism or collectivism (see *EG*, sections 189 and 240). But Francis's apostolic exhortation has little or nothing positive to say about the market economy (see section 204 for an overwrought denunciation of "the unseen forces and the invisible hand of the market"). Rather than emphasizing social and political measures to ameliorate poverty and help the poorest of the poor, the pope endorses government action to promote "a better distribution of income" (*EG*, 204).

This is undoubtedly in some tension with his support of subsidiarity. A state dedicated to full-scale redistribution will hardly respect decentralization and local initiatives. Pope Francis insists that he is not "proposing an irresponsible populism," a recognition on his part that there can be a demagoguery that speaks irresponsibly in the name of the poor (think of the devastation wrought by Chavist socialism in Venezuela since the late 1990s). His anti-capitalism is thus qualified in important respects. In one passing remark, he grudgingly acknowledges the legitimacy of private property if it serves larger "social" purposes (*EG*, 189). Yet he also insists that solidarity "must be lived as the decision to restore to the poor what belongs to them." Such language might be misconstrued to justify "irresponsible populism" of the kind that has nearly destroyed Venezuela. The pope thus goes back and forth between theological to sociopolitical affirmations, an oscillation that has given rise to ideological readings of his intention on the part of many journalists and politicians. But the pope insists that his remarks owe nothing to "personal interest or political ideology." Instead, he wishes to liberate souls from becoming enthralled to "an individualistic, indifferent and self-centered mentality." He wishes to encourage "a way of living and thinking which is more humane, noble and fruitful, and which will bring dignity" to men's "presence on earth" (*EG*, section 208). That is surely an inherent part of Christian wisdom and of true evangelization. But it must be added that the pope's remarkably undisciplined off-the-cuff remarks, filled with vitriol for the market economy and Western "capitalism" in general, do little to honor these distinctions.

Pope Francis proffers many prudential judgments that Catholics and other thoughtful men of good will might disagree with. I have already noted his disturbing tendency to ignore or underplay the Church's age-old opposition to political utopianism and its concerns about the threat that many versions of socialism pose to human freedom and dignity. At the same time, Pope Francis's reflection on the social dimensions of the Gospel is careful to reaffirm the Church's dual emphasis on solidarity and the necessity of affirming the civic common good, and subsidiarity and the necessity of avoiding collectivist policies that undermine the social, civic, and economic initiatives that properly belong to a self-governing civil society. Those are surely the heart of his message, read in light of the larger tradition of Catholic social teaching.

The pope rightly strikes a note of modesty regarding the supposed comprehensiveness—and infallibility—of the Church's practical recommendations to the state and civil society: "The Church does not have solutions for every particular issue." He leaves to thoughtful laymen the task of discerning "those programs which best respond to the dignity of each person and the common good" (*EG*, 241). It is thus best to interpret this apostolic exhortation in light of age-old Christian wisdom and the fuller insights of the Catholic social tradition since Pope Leo inaugurated it in 1891. We must take Pope Francis at his word. He is not simply an ideologist, nor does he advocate, at least most of the time, "unruly activism." His own prudential judgments are sometimes interesting and worthy of respectful consideration. But they are not coextensive with Christian political wisdom.

It must be added that the pope errs when he states that "authentic Islam and the proper reading of the Koran are opposed to every form of violence" (*EG*, section 253). This is a rare concession to political correctness, pure and simple. Mohammed murdered many infidels, including the defenseless Jews of Medina. He was a warrior as well as a religious figure. And authentic Islam endorses *jihad of the sword*, even if it is not the only or highest meaning of *jihad* or struggle in the Koran or the Islamic tradition. Pope Francis's larger point remains. Muslim countries are morally obliged "to grant Christians freedom to worship and to practice their faith, in light of the freedom which followers of Islam enjoy in Western countries!" (*EG*, section 253). Nothing is gained, however, by obfuscating the troubling fact that "violent fundamentalism" (*EG*, section 253) finds some justification in "authentic Islam." Islam has never been a "religion of peace," a fact fully acknowledged by Pope Benedict XVI in his 2007 Regensburg Address.

THE CHURCH AND EUROPE

The future and destiny of the Christian faith has always been tied to the future and destiny of Europe. Christianity became a truly "universal" religion when St. Paul crossed over to Macedonia to bring the "good news" to the Greeks (*Acts* 16: 6–10). Like St. Peter, St. Paul died in Rome, the "eternal city" that would become the symbol and embodiment of the inescapable catholicity of the Christian faith. Prior to Pope Francis, all those who have held the See of Peter have been Europeans (the Argentinian Bergoglio is himself of Italian descent and speaks Italian as one of his native languages). The Church is inescapably Eurocentric and at the same time inescapably universalistic, in part due to the providential encounter of the Church with Greek philosophy and Roman culture, as Pope John Paul II pointed out in his rich 1999 encyclical *Fides et Ratio*. The Church cannot be indifferent to the fate of European liberty, of the encounter of the Christian proposition with the first civilization that truly learned to speak of man as man. If Christianity is in the process of losing its European sources of vitality, as Pope John Paul II and Pope Benedict XVI both feared, then this would be an immeasurable loss for both Europe and the integrity of the Christian religion. Much is at stake in the Christian religion's continuing ability to inform Europe's practice of liberty and its understanding of human dignity.

Pope Francis's fullest articulation of the relationship between Christianity and Europe can be found in his November 25, 2014, address to the European parliament. There he evokes the speech that Pope John Paul II had given to the same forum more than a quarter of a century earlier. Pope Francis notes that Europe is now whole and free, and that the division into "opposing blocs" is a thing of the past (although abundant tensions surely remain between East and West). Like John Paul II, Pope Francis suggests that the defense of the dignity of the human person is unthinkable without Christianity and the multiple ways in which it has helped "shape an awareness of the unique worth of each individual person." Modern Europe must learn not only from "recent events" (the totalitarian denial of human liberty and dignity in the twentieth century) but also from Christianity's "transcendent" affirmation of the human person. The relational person, as opposed to the autonomous individual, owes much to the age-old Christian encounter with European cultures. In some memorable passages, the pope argues that there can be no true dignity if human thought and religious liberty are repressed, if the rule of law does not provide a bulwark against tyranny (it might have helped to speak these words in Cuba, too). He defends the social preconditions of human dignity, rooted as they are in guaranteeing the basic needs of the individual and of employment that makes possible dignified work.

Like his immediate predecessors, Pope Francis defends human rights against the encroachments of a tyrannical state. Like Popes John Paul II and Benedict XVI, he also criticizes the "misuse" of the concept of human rights, a growing tendency in advanced intellectual circles to sever the human person from "all social and anthropological concepts" that inform the exercise of human freedom. The individual must be linked to the civic common good and to the full array of intermediate groups, including families and churches, which give content to human freedom. Severed from all notions of a "greater good," appeals to the pure autonomy of human rights can readily become new sources "of conflicts and violence." The human person, so understood, is quite distinct from the "monadic" and willful individual.

In one of the best passages in the speech, Pope Francis connects "transcendent human dignity" to an understanding of an enduring human nature that is informed by the "innate" human capacity "to distinguish good from evil." This is the traditional wisdom of the Church and the "perennial philosophy" that has accompanied it for a millennium. Alluding to St. Paul, Pope Francis speaks of a "compass" within our hearts, which "God has impressed upon all creation"—thus appealing to "natural law" without explicitly using that term. At least on this occasion, Pope Francis seems to appreciate that the Catholic Church remains the best spiritual and institutional vehicle for the defense of the natural moral law and that it needs to remind Europe and the world of old wisdom.

The pope emphatically states that human freedom is not "absolute," but always refers to "beings in relation." This is a clear affirmation of the personalism that informs his sociopolitical reflection. Today, that understanding of human freedom and dignity is threatened by a technology that escapes moral-political control (Francis habitually refers to a "throwaway culture" that readily disposes of persons and things). If Europe is to remain faithful to "the centrality of the human person," she must remain open to "the transcendent"; Europe must then continue to recognize the contribution that Christianity makes to "a humanism centered on respect for the dignity of the human person." Christianity's role must not be relegated to the distant past if Europe is to remain true to itself.

However, one of the troubling lacunae of this address is the failure of the pontiff to even refer to the European nation as the home of self-government and free and dignified political life. Strikingly, there is no mention in his address of France, Italy, Germany, or Poland—or any other European nation. Pope Francis rightly warns against a conception of the European Union that would emphasize unity at the expense of legitimate diversity. He defends the "diversity proper to each people, cherishing particular traditions, acknowledging its past history and its roots." He evokes subsidiarity. But he never speaks of the political form that is the nation. He never speaks of the nation proper, the concretized political form that is the home of the very traditions that he rightly says must be safeguarded today.

It was Churchill, after all, who argued at Zurich on September 19, 1946, that European unity could only be built on reconciliation and cooperation between a "spiritually great France" and a "spiritually great Germany." There is no Europe, or European Union, without the self-governing nation. As the French Catholic political philosopher Pierre Manent has suggestively argued in *Beyond Radical Secularism*, for all its imperfections, the European nation allowed Christians "to govern oneself by the guidance of one's own reason and with attention to grace." It allowed "for the collaboration of human prudence and divine Providence." It is thus all the more regrettable that the contemporary Church is prone to invoking a "world governing authority"—even as it ritualistically appeals to "subsidiarity" as one of its animating principles. The Church needs to relearn the language of humane national loyalty, a language that cannot be confused with the kind of toxic and pagan nationalism that abhors the Christian proposition and genuine human universality.

Once again, Pope Francis speaks ominously about "uniform systems of economic power at the service of unseen empires." Some of this is unduly sinister; some of it reflects perfectly legitimate concerns about unchecked globalization. His language is vague and subject to ideological appropriation. Repeating some of the ecological themes that have been central to his papacy, Pope Francis emphasizes, quite properly, that "each of us has a personal responsibility to care for creation." In the best Catholic tradition, he reminds us that we are "stewards, but not masters" of nature. Lamentably, however, Pope Francis here shows no awareness that increasingly, in the form of depth ecology, environmentalism has sometimes become a "secular religion" shorn of all forms of Christian humanism. Christians are called "to enjoy and use properly nature." They are never called to deify it or make it an idol in place of the transcendent God.

Finally, the pope treats "the question of migration" as a strictly humanitarian concern. "We cannot allow the Mediterranean to become a vast cemetery!" That point is undoubtedly true. But it is not enough. Francis's address to the European parliament does not address legitimate questions of security in an age marked by terrorism, nor does it recognize that the West could be fundamentally transformed by allowing millions of Muslims, mainly young men (and some markedly unfriendly to Western "values") to enter a Europe which has not wholly left behind its fruitful encounter and engagement with Christianity. He does not seem to worry about the myriad consequences of Europe losing its "Christian mark" altogether. And in his ill-disciplined, off-the-cuff remarks on this subject, Pope Francis rarely distinguishes between migrants searching for a better standard of living and genuine refugees fleeing war and religious and political persecution.

Statesmen, even Catholic statesmen, must weigh and balance the full array of legitimate social and political concerns. Their decisions cannot be ruled wholly by humanitarian considerations or by a sentimentality that abstracts from difficult truths and decisions. The question of migration cannot be completely severed from the question of Islam, particularly radical Islam. For this reason, the discussion of migration is the least persuasive part of Pope Francis's speech because it abstracts almost wholly from the perspective of the responsible statesman. That perspective must inform Catholic social teaching if it is to avoid becoming a form of what Alexis de Tocqueville derided as "literary politics."

THE CHURCH AND AMERICA

The United States is the world's most successful experiment in democratic self-government and a bulwark, for good or for ill, of international order. The United States led resistance to the worst forms of totalitarianism in the twentieth century. It also has a large and vibrant (if declining) Catholic community and provides a disproportionate share of the resources that are necessary for the Church to carry out her responsibilities in the world. What is more, the United States is increasingly a laboratory for the unfolding of both the best and worst features of liberty in the modern world. The Church therefore cannot remain silent about America or the American proposition that "all men are created equal" (in the memorable words of the Declaration of Independence). Pope Francis's "Address to a Joint Session of the United States Congress" on September 24, 2015, accordingly is important, both as a judgment about the American proposition and as a statement of how the Church understands Christian engagement in the contemporary world.

In his address to Congress, Pope Francis acknowledges that democracy "is deeply rooted in the mind of the American people." He invokes the inviolable dignity of the human person and cites the "self-evident truths" of the Declaration of Independence as an example of a politics truly "at the service of the human person." He also points out the myriad affinities that exist between what it means to be a Catholic and what it means to be an American. But he also again warns against politics becoming "a slave to the economy and finance." The pope fashions a vision of the political common good in which "particular interests" are sacrificed "in order to share, in justice and peace, its goods, its interests, its social life."

Perhaps this is a too-lofty goal, since the common interest should never run roughshod over the full variety of legitimate individual and group interests. What seems to be missing is a conception of politics that knows how to reconcile individual rights with a substantial conception of a shared or common good—a conception of politics for which the classical and Christian traditions of moral and political reflection provide ample resources.

It should be added that the pope acknowledges, as he had already done in *Laudato Si'*, that "business is a noble vocation" (*LS*, 129), that it can aid in the fight against poverty and in the creation and distribution of wealth. In an important affirmation, he states that "the right use of natural resources, the proper application of technology and the harnessing of the spirit of enterprise are essential elements of an economy which seeks to be modern, inclusive and sustainable." At least in this passage, Pope Francis is no Luddite; he does not pine for an economic order that escapes the challenges of modernity. He does not see any fundamental opposition between "the spirit of enterprise" and the environmental stewardship that is necessary for the proper care of our "common home." Francis's anti-capitalist rhetoric, on fiery display in the speeches he delivered in Latin America earlier in 2015, is considerably muted in this address. (One heard little about the "nobility" of business or the essential place of the "spirit of enterprise" when Francis fulminated against "demonic" capitalism in Bolivia and elsewhere.) In any case, in his speech to Congress the pope's rhetoric on political economy is balanced and at the service of a genuinely humane economy.

Pope Francis pays eloquent tribute to four exemplary Americans: Abraham Lincoln's defense of liberty and equality and his struggle against slavery and for a "new birth of freedom" in the aftermath of the Civil War; Martin Luther King's struggle for racial justice and "liberty in plurality and non-exclusion"; Dorothy Day's quest for "social justice"; and Thomas Merton's "capacity for dialogue and openness to God." There is much to be recommended in the lives and struggles of these four great Americans— though it must also be noted that Dorothy Day's admirable work for the poor was accompanied by a troubling vitriolic hostility to a market economy and a militant pacifism that denied the legitimacy of self-defense against totalitarian aggression. In this regard, she was not faithful to the full range of Catholic social teaching. That teaching does not recommend pacifism and does not condemn the market economy in principle. As we have already noted, in a 2017 book of interviews with the French social scientist Dominique Wolton, Pope Francis comes very close to questioning the continuing validity of the "just war" tradition. This would entail a fundamental challenge to the idea of the political common good (and the responsibilities of statesmen) and would allow evil and tyranny to run rampant in the world. It is, of course, highly doubtful that any pope has the authority to modify the permanent principles and basic moral framework that inform authentic political judgment. The weight of Christian wisdom is broader and deeper than the private judgments, highly idiosyncratic in this case, of this or any other pope.

The pope uses this occasion to denounce "every type of fundamentalism" that gives rise to violence and "ideological extremism." He knows that religion can be appropriated by extremists, but he fails, perhaps out of undue ecumenical sensitivity, to mention the Islamist extremism that is the source of so many "brutal atrocities" today. He warns against "simple reductionism which sees only good and evil." He is right to criticize that kind of moral fanaticism, uninformed as it is by charity and a humanizing recognition of the complexity of the soul.

Regrettably, however, the Holy Father says nothing about the scourge of our time in the prosperous and democratic West, a debilitating moral relativism that denies evil and sin and collaborates with political correctness in all its forms. Surely, what Pope Benedict XVI called "the dictatorship of relativism" is a grave threat to American and democratic liberty and to the integrity of souls in the contemporary world. The failure to mention the threat of relativism is a missed opportunity and seemingly reflects a diminished commitment to an unchanging natural moral law.

The pope speaks of the Golden Rule ("Do unto others as you would have them do unto you") and reminds us of our "responsibility to protect and defend human life at every stage of its development." While he is silent, except by inference, about the grave and intrinsic evil of abortion, the killing of the defenseless and innocent unborn, he does state that his own fidelity to the Golden Rule has led him, from the beginning of his ministry, "to advocate at different levels for the global abolition of the death penalty." Here he ignores the teaching of scripture and tradition on this matter. *The Catechism of the Catholic Church* explicitly states in its section on punishment the "right and duty of legitimate public authority" to punish crimes of "extreme gravity" with the "death penalty" (*CC*, 2266), even as it states a preference for "bloodless means" where they are feasible, since such means "better correspond to the concrete means of the common good" (*CC*, 2267). Francis's opposition to the death penalty in all cases seems to be rooted in "an emerging global awareness" that he appeals to in his 2016 book of interviews, *In the Name of Mercy*. That appeal is humanitarian and historicist— that is, not specifically Catholic—and is a striking example of Francis's tendency to conflate the Gospel with the requirements of a humanitarian moral message. This is perhaps the gravest failing of his pontificate, one that bodes ill for the future of the Church and its ability to moderate democratic modernity's drift to softness and relativism. He comes close to "kneeling before the world," to cite once again Jacques Maritain's prophetic warning in *The Peasant of the Garonne* to the post-Vatican II Church.

Pope Francis came to the United States to minister to his flock and to speak at the World Congress of Families in Philadelphia. Near the end of his address to Congress, he expressed his concerns for the integrity of the family and noted that it is "threatened, perhaps, as never before, from within and without." This makes it all the more striking that he chose to remain silent here about the judicial imposition of same-sex marriage in all 50 American states. His silence was disheartening, particularly for those who remain faithful to Church teaching on this matter and to the requirements of "natural law" and "right reason." Pope Francis risked nothing from our reigning elites in condemning the death penalty; by contrast, a fulsome denunciation of abortion on demand and the reconstitution of marriage to allow "same-sex marriage" would not have gone over well with those who somewhat incoherently describe themselves as "Pope Francis Catholics." At a minimum, an opportunity was lost to clarify Catholic teaching and to educate Americans about the enduring moral foundations of democracy and civil society.

IN THE NAME OF MERCY

Pope Francis has placed extraordinary emphasis on the proclamation of God's mercy. He has published a book of conversations on this theme with

Andrea Tornielli, titled *The Name of God Is Mercy* (it has appeared in all the major languages). In the spring of 2015, he announced an Extraordinary Jubilee of Mercy—a year of mercy beginning on December 8, 2015 (the Feast of the Immaculate Conception), and continuing through November 20, 2016 (the Feast of Christ the King). In his conversations with Tornielli, he speaks of a humanity that is "deeply wounded" by the effects of "original sin." Man needs the mercy of a gracious God. Humankind knows how to distinguish good and evil, "but we often fall because of our weaknesses and choose evil." The pope acknowledges that modern man has largely "lost its sense of sin" (he quotes Pius XII to that effect) and that he often succumbs to a relativism where "all things seem equal, all things appear the same." This is one of the very rare references to relativism that can be found in the writings and addresses of Pope Francis. The Church has a responsibility to condemn sin, to relay the truth "this is a sin." At the same time, it must be a vehicle for "the infinite mercy of God." The welcoming home of the prodigal son is the heart of the "good news" that the Gospel proclaims.

The Holy Father rarely speaks of repentance. As the German Catholic philosopher Robert Spaemann has written, Pope Francis sometimes "gets ahead of God's mercy." Reiterating his earlier controversial remarks about homosexual people ("Who Am I to Judge?") he rightly speaks of the need to treat homosexuals with delicacy and prevent them from being "marginalized." But there is no talk of abstinence or the forswearing of sin. He, of course, would "prefer that homosexuals come to confession." But repentance is not emphasized as a precondition for engagement with the life of the Church. There is a larger problem here. The emphasis on the gratuitous love of God seems to crowd out the repentance that is the precondition for the soul's receptivity to divine grace and mercy. In a relativistic age, people are prone to take God's grace for granted, to assume that sin isn't truly sinful, that it doesn't distance the human person from the light of God. Mercy risks becoming thoughtlessly identified with democratic relativism where one loses a sense of objective right and wrong.

Pope Francis has interesting and important things to say about sin, relativism, and divine mercy. But he does not put these insights together. He does not seem to have reflected on the way democratic relativism poses an insuperable obstacle to the soul's encounter with a loving God. As we have already noted, he thinks mercy can overcome even the most "serious misdeeds and terrible crimes." But mercy cannot do its work without repentance, and repentance doesn't eliminate the need for earthly justice as a divinely ordained instrument of the common good.

The pope does not explicitly acknowledge the difference between a Christianity that recognizes the legitimate place of punishment and a secular humanitarian ethos that is guided by free-floating compassion. Divine mercy is not humanitarian compassion. It is not a substitute for personal repentance and the firm, if humane, exercise of the rule of law. If one "gets ahead of God's mercy," one risks reinforcing the tragedy of the age: the denial of sin, evil, and personal responsibility. The evocation of divine mercy must never reinforce what Pope Benedict XVI called "the dictatorship of relativism." These are undoubtedly matters that call forth reflection and discernment on the part of all faithful Christians.

THE FAMILY IN THE MODERN WORLD

Released in the spring of 2016, Pope Francis's latest major statement to the Church and the world is an apostolic exhortation on love in the family, *Amoris Laetitia*. It does not directly concern the Church's social teaching, although what the pope says about contemporary threats to the integrity of the family is directly relevant to any reflection on his contribution to Catholic social teaching (see *AL*, section 53, where Pope Francis speaks of ongoing efforts in "many countries" to "legally deconstruct" the family on models "based almost exclusively on the autonomy of the individual will"). Much of this apostolic exhortation is quite traditional in character, and is in accord with the age-old teaching of the Church. Pope Francis engages in a beautiful exegesis of what scripture has to say about the family. His reading of St. Paul's famous hymn to love in *I Corinthians* is one of the highlights of this document. Both insightful and lyrical, this discussion prepares the way for a luminous discussion of conjugal love, "the love between husband and wife, a love sanctified, enriched and illuminated by the grace of the sacrament of marriage" (*AL*, section 95). However, the pope's discussion is marred by a tendency to redefine Christian family life in terms of "values" (*AL*, section 35) that the Church presents to the world. The Church's teaching is presented as a "demanding ideal" (*AL*, section 38) of which fallible men will necessarily fall short.

The pope acknowledges that the Church's teaching on marriage and the family is countercultural and that the Church can "hardly stop advocating marriage simply to avoid countering contemporary sensibilities" (*AL*, section 35). But he seems to want to meet the world halfway, all in the name of "compassion" and the recognition of the "frailty of individuals like the Samaritan woman or the woman caught in adultery" (*AL*, section 38). The Church must not "desist from proposing the full ideal of marriage" in a world marked by moral indifference and "relativism" (*AL*, section 307). Yet by redefining the Church's teaching on the good life in terms of amorphous "values" and "ideals," the pope moves far away from the Church's traditional categories of "goods" and "virtues." He assumes an unbridgeable gap between the ideal and reality, thus leaving much room, perhaps too much room, for pastoral discernment in dealing with cases of adultery and divorce and remarriage (*AL*, especially note 351). To cite Spaemann again, Pope Francis risks getting ahead of God's mercy when he asks the Church to forgive or overlook objectively sinful moral choices and conditions, and this without repentance or a change in the sinner's behavior. The pope acknowledges that it is wrong to place the unions of homosexuals "on the same level as marriage" (*AL*, section 251). "There are absolutely no grounds for considering homosexual unions to be in any way similar or remotely analogous to God's plan for marriage and family" (*AL*, section 251). But the same misplaced compassion for the divorced and remarried could readily lead to "pastoral" accommodation of "homosexual unions" in the name of compassion and mercy. Once again, Pope Francis tends to conflate divine mercy and democratic compassion. He claims fidelity to the "ideal," if that is indeed the right way to describe fidelity to the Gospel and the moral law, even as he risks accommodating objective situations of sin.

The pope and his acolytes scorn the "legalism" of those such as Cardinal Burke, and the other issuers of the famous "dubia," who ask for nothing more than doctrinal and moral clarity about the teaching of the Church. By doing so, they sow confusion among the faithful and give in to the pressures of the secular world. In the summer of 2017, Pope Francis dismissed Cardinal Gerhard Muller of the Congregation for the Defense of the Faith for reiterating the Church's age-old teaching on marriage and for interpreting *Amoris Laetitia* in light of that teaching. Muller had argued openly that no pope (or "angel" or "council") has the authority to change the fundamental teachings of the Church. This pontificate is thus increasingly disheartening for those who remain faithful to the traditional teaching of the Church and the requirements of the natural moral law. Francis has left the Church divided and vulnerable to an unthinking political correctness. One suspects this is not what the papal conclave had in mind when this Argentinian pope was elected in April 2013.

CONCLUSION

There is wisdom and insight to be found in the writings, speeches, and addresses of Pope Francis. He is at his best when he thinks and writes in continuity with the full weight of Christian wisdom and with the insights of his immediate predecessors. But when he departs from them, he tends to confuse humanitarian concerns with properly Christian ones. He tends to give a one-sided "progressivist" reading of Catholic social teaching, radicalizing the Church's criticisms of the market economy and failing to reiterate its serious reservations about socialism in its various forms. Remarkably, he seems to have learned very little about the gravest evil of the twentieth century—totalitarianism—hence his troubling indulgence toward Communist tyranny in Cuba. Perhaps he needs to pay more attention to the experiences of John Paul II with totalitarian Communism and Pope Benedict XVI with Nazi barbarism (he seems to be remarkably unaffected by his two great predecessors). If he did so, he would not see liberal capitalism as an unmitigated evil, as he often does, especially in his extemporaneous remarks. Pope Francis likes to emphasize those parts of Catholic teaching that are uncontroversial with left-liberal elites. His appeals to Catholic social teaching tend to be selective. It is all the more important, then, that his statements and writings be read in the context of the tradition as a whole, and not the other way around. One is well advised to follow a "hermeneutic of continuity" in approaching the thought of this and other popes. And it is imperative to resist the tendency to identify Catholic wisdom with a secular humanitarianism that lacks both intellectual clarity and moral rigor. So much will be lost if the Church continues to "kneel before the world."

• SOURCES AND SUGGESTED READINGS •

Pope Francis's *Praise Be to You [Laudato Si']: On Care for Our Common Home* is available in a beautiful edition from Ignatius Press (San Francisco, 2015). In evaluating the encyclical, I have drawn upon the lucid and penetrating analysis by James V. Schall, S. J., "Concerning the 'Ecological' Path to Salvation," *Catholic World Report,*

June 21, 2015. On the pathologies of the Argentinian model of political and economic development, see George F. Will, "Pope Francis's fact-free flamboyance," *Washington Post*, September 18, 2015.

The most accessible version of *The Joy of the Gospel* (*Evangelii Gaudium*) is the one available from Image Books (New York, 2013). The best Catholic engagement with Islam and Islamism remains Pope Benedict XVI's September 2006 Regensburg Address. For a suggestive commentary (and accompanying text of the address) see James V. Schall, *The Regensburg Lecture* (South Bend, IN: St. Augustine's Press, 2007).

Pope Francis's address to the European parliament of November 25, 2014, can be found online at *America* magazine, November 25, 2014. The Pope's address to the American Congress of September 24, 2015, can be found in *Pope Francis Speaks to the United States and Cuba: Speeches, Homilies, and Interviews* (Huntington, IN: Our Sunday Visitor Press, 2015), pp. 79–88. See Pierre Manent's *Beyond Radical Secularism*, translated by Ralph C. Hancock, introduction by Daniel J. Mahoney (South Bend, IN: St. Augustine's Press, 2016) for a particularly penetrating discussion of the "Christian mark" of the European nation.

The Pope's most ample discussion of mercy can be found in Pope Francis, *The Name of God Is Mercy: A Conversation with Andrea Tornielli* (New York: Random House, 2016). *Amoris Laetitia: On Love in the Family* is available in a readable and accessible version from Our Sunday Visitor Press (2016). The full text of Robert Spaemann's interview about *Amoris Laetitia* and "getting ahead of God's mercy" can be found at the website of the Catholic News Agency, April 29, 2016.

John Allen (*Crux*, September 13, 2017) provides a helpful discussion of Pope Francis's occasional acknowledgment that a genuinely political approach to immigration requires "prudence" as well as "heart." But much of the time, Francis appears to be an advocate of porous, if not "open," borders. He seemingly pays only lip service to concerns about integration and common citizenship.

For Pope Francis's flirtation with pacifism, see Pope Francis (Pape François), *Rencontres avec Dominique Wolton, Politique et société* (Paris: Éditions de l'Observatoire, 2017), pp. 57–58. Francis asserts on p. 58 that "no war is just" and that "the only just thing is peace." He seems not to have contemplated the possibility of an unjust peace, "the peace of the grave." His analysis lacks both moral and political seriousness and attentiveness to the Catechism or the Catholic tradition.

CHAPTER SEVEN

Jürgen Habermas and the Postpolitical Temptation

Throughout this book, we have emphasized the inherent connection between humanitarianism and the post-political or post-national impulse. In this chapter, we will examine the relationship between the European project in its dominant form and the humanitarian civil religion promoted by the likes of Jürgen Habermas. Let us begin at the beginning.

The European project, as it is called, is marked by great promise and great peril. No less than Winston Churchill called for the reconciliation of a "spiritually great France" and a "spiritually great Germany" in a memorable address in Zurich in September 1946. Churchill foresaw a "United States of Europe" that could bring peace, prosperity, and liberty to a continent that had been ravaged by war and tyranny. He imagined Britain as a friendly onlooker of this process of European pacification and unification, wishing Europe well while remaining committed to Britain's empire and commonwealth and to her "special relationship" with the United States.

In his recent book *The Lure of Technology* (New York: Polity Press, 2015), the famous German philosopher and social theorist Jürgen Habermas invokes the authority of Winston Churchill to encourage an overcoming of "national particularisms," first in Europe and then in the world as a whole. As this book reveals, Habermas is *the* theorist of post-national democracy, of a "postnational world order." Churchill was, of course, attached to Britain and fought heroically to protect her sovereignty and liberty, even as he foresaw the benefits of much wider circles of cooperation and collective security. He appreciated the promise of European unity. Still, it is far from clear that he would endorse Habermas's dream of a transnational world society. For Habermas, the nation is in the end an atavism, an anachronism, and it will survive in diminished form only if it jettisons stubborn claims to sovereignty and autonomy.

Habermas claims to be a partisan of a truly political Europe, but his conception of politics is remarkably bloodless and abstract. The title essay in this volume of essays, interviews, and public interventions diagnoses the excessively technocratic character of contemporary "Europe" in thoughtful and helpful ways. Habermas appreciates that the "new technocratic form of cooperation" that animates the European Council and the collective European response to the banking and sovereign debt crisis after 2008 suffers from a serious democratic deficit. The European project has relied for too long on the passive support of the peoples of Europe; it has done little or nothing to give shape to a properly European "will-formation" (one notices how inelegant Habermas's formulations sometimes are). He has little patience for the claim that European nations are the signatories to the European treaties, culminating in the Treaty of Lisbon in 2007. National autonomy is a "fiction." A truly political Europe must therefore strive to overcome it.

To be sure, he is entirely right about the limits of a "technocracy without democratic roots." But his vision of a transnational or supranational Europe is chiefly informed by a desire to preserve the welfare state in its present form (with its ever-expanding "social rights") against a capitalism that he deplores. He tellingly abstracts from foreign policy—it doesn't seem to belong to his conception of politics—and is completely silent about the threat that radical Islam poses to the integrity of Europe.

Habermas presents his readers with a stark choice between "democracy or capitalism," which is the title of one of the book's essays. A transnational Europe, the avant-garde of a transnational world society, is "indispensable if unbridled global capitalism is to be steered into socially acceptable channels." Political globalization, on a massive scale, is thus the only alternative to economic globalization. It is the vehicle of social justice or solidarity, which Habermas always identifies with a robust statism. He never acknowledges that the requirements of economic competition and economic growth are legitimate goods in a liberal society, goods that have to be weighed against the social rights that are at the core of his political vision. In Habermas's Europe there will be no place for prudential judgment, with all its complexities and competing demands, which weighs and balances market freedoms with the full array of social security measures. For him, the latter are rights that can brook no significant limit or qualification. They are, in decisive respects, beyond discussion and will be codified and ratified by European law.

But Habermas does not rest content with the evolutionary transfer of sovereign rights to an enhanced European entity. The new Europe will establish joint fiscal, budgetary, and (redistributive) economic policy. It will harmonize social policy across the whole of Europe. In doing so, "the red line of the classical understanding of sovereignty would be crossed." Europeans would abandon the "fiction" that "the nation-states are 'the sovereign subjects' of the European Treaties," beginning with the Treaty of Rome in 1957, which established the European Community, and culminating in the Treaty of Lisbon in 2007, which solidified the vision of a postnational Europe. To renounce this vision would be to "turn one's back on world history," a history that he believes is leaving the nation definitively behind. He provides no real evidence for this claim.

In what way would a Habermasian Europe be a political Europe? His European legislators would transform "the claims to solidarity of the marginalized...into social rights." His vision thus presumes a direction to history (characterized by ever more "social emancipation" and tutelary government). These questions are beyond dispute for Habermas. To some, this will look like the "soft despotism" famously invoked by Tocqueville at the end of *Democracy in America*. To others, it will merely codify the European model of the "providential state," as the French revealingly call it. In any case, it is hardly a model of politics in which informed citizens debate great and contentious questions. Where is the partisan conflict that is inevitable in genuinely political life?

I am not arguing in principle against social rights or modest protectionism and other hedges against the effects of globalization. That I'll leave to the doctrinaires of economic liberalism. But these rights invoked by Habermas are not absolute, and their articulation and expansion alone do not provide politics with a meaningful content. In Habermas's supranational construct, nations still exist, but they are completely subordinate to European law. Indeed, he argues with some justification that this is, for all intents and purposes, already the case. European officials would be chosen by European voters as a whole—forever putting an end to the "fiction" of national self-government. Of course, the remnant of the nation would still have a "monopoly of legitimate violence," to cite Weber's classic definition, striving to protect "the emancipatory achievements of their respective national democracies." Here again, the nation is reduced to a vehicle for protecting (ever-expanding) social rights and the memory of the "revolutionary past." This is not nothing. But Habermas reduces the founding moments of European democracy to 1789 and 1968: respectively, the eruption of a national vehicle for the "rights of man"—no matter how destructive the French Revolution was of liberty in its concrete forms—and that real and symbolic moment of social unrest when Europeans began challenging political and social authority in all its forms. Habermas makes no mention of the millennia-old European nation with its roots in the High Middle Ages. The conserving, as opposed to emancipatory, dimensions of rich European national traditions are passed by. Christianity is given some credit for defending human dignity and for giving genuine substance to secular calls for human solidarity. But in the end Christianity, and what Pierre Manent calls the "nation of a Christian mark," are thoroughly dispensable. Ultimately, Habermas is a partisan of what he calls the "secular religion of humanity." Like his hero Heinrich Heine, Habermas hopes and offers a secular prayer that "ridiculous national prejudices are disappearing." His heart is with the "emphatic unity of democracy, human rights, cosmopolitan hope, and pacifism," culminating in a great project of social emancipation. That is the antinomian significance of 1968 in Habermas's social and political vision for Europe and Germany. He has little respect for Adenauer's dignified, conservative postwar Republic, which was still rooted in the German and European past, with its evocation of "Christian democracy" and its straightforward anti-Communism. (Habermas rightly despises Hitler and all his works but is seemingly more ambivalent about Communist totalitarianism, the evils of which he rarely mentions.)

After the failed European revolutions of 1848, Heine broke with political utopianism and even became a believer of sorts in God. But Habermas assures us that if Heine gave up on an "extravagant idea of Revolution," he remained faithful to the "political enforcement of human rights, the 'Ten Commandments of the new world faith.'" But are rights enough to give human and political life meaning? Are the moral contents of life reducible to rights claims, important as they are in the fight against tyranny? Rights may constrain politics, but they cannot be the substance of politics, which always turns on the question of what kind of people we wish to be.

Conservative-minded statesmen such as Churchill and de Gaulle still saw the old nation (and in de Gaulle's case, the old religion) as pillars of a Europe worthy of the name. However, Habermas is too confident in the philosophy of history to doubt the triumph of emancipatory cosmopolitanism. Perhaps churchmen who invoke the necessity and inevitability of a "governing world authority"—a claim made in several papal social encyclicals since the 1960s—should think long and hard about the philosophy of history and the "secular religion" that will provide the inevitable spiritual underpinning of a transnational global society. The nation is, and remains, the political form of the Christian West, and more thought needs to be given to the political and spiritual costs of saying adieu to the political form that made self-government and spiritual communion possible. The West did not begin in 1968. The European project will only remain viable if it draws all the proper conclusions from this fact.

All this said, Habermas's fundamental decency needs to be acknowledged. He is a man of peace and reason. He can write respectfully about such diverse figures as Martin Buber and his Jewish philosophy of dialogue (in a beautiful talk at the Hebrew University in Jerusalem, reproduced in this volume) and Leo Strauss and his recovery of classical political philosophy (in a thought-provoking essay on the reception of Jewish thinkers in post-1945 Germany). He is no Badiou or Žižek, justifying the unjustifiable ("the idea of Communism," and Stalin and Mao, too, in their cases). No doubt there are worse things than Kant-inspired cosmopolitanism, even if it needs to be challenged by a richer and more capacious sense of political possibility and limitation.

Habermas is the theorist of "communicative rationality" and a "discourse" theory that is barely accessible to the uninitiated. But in the post-national Europe and post-national world society he envisions, both politics and the higher manifestations of the soul would atrophy. That is a paradox that ought to give one pause.

CHAPTER EIGHT

Reason, Conscience, and the Return to Truth

This entire work presupposes that human beings have "reasonable" access to an order of things above the human will. With the help of Pope emeritus Benedict XVI and Cardinal Newman, this concluding chapter will explore conscience or the "listening heart" of scripture as a trustworthy portal to a non-arbitrary order of truth and justice. Conscience, so understood, is at the very heart of civilization worthy of the name.

For more than a century and a half, the specter of secularization has haunted the West. At the beginning of the twentieth century, Max Weber famously spoke of the "disenchantment of the world." He premised a "rationalization" of the world where "facts" and values" were definitively separated and where "the great enchanted garden" of religious societies was inexorably replaced by a cold and soulless reason. In truth, there was little reason in the traditional sense in Weberian rationality. Reason, in his understanding, could say nothing, absolutely nothing, about the meaning of life. Nor could reason provide any substantive guidance for moral and political choices. Weber was a proto-existentialist, a "scholar" who did not quite succumb to Nietzschean nihilism (witness his faith in an austere and methodologically rigorous social science). And he presupposed rather arbitrarily that the world before disenchantment was ruled by "magic" in various forms, and not, at least in the West, by a capacious reason that coexisted with faith in the divine source or ground of the "natural order of things."

Spiritually discerning poets provide a better guide to a West haunted by the "death of God." In his famous 1867 poem "Dover Beach," the English writer Matthew Arnold spoke regretfully about the "melancholy, long, withdrawing roar" of "The Sea of Faith," a withdrawal he lamented even if he could not affirm the truth of faith. Arnold placed his hopes in "love," in the human capacity to "be true to one another!" This is not nothing, but it is, in the end, rather thin gruel. Arnold's accompanying faith in "culture," in a conservative version of liberal humanism, protected him from the temptation of nihilism, even if it offered nothing in the way of a renewal of a robust conception of reason and faith. His was a politics of cultural lament. The great twentieth-century Polish poet Czesław Miłosz refused to jettison faith as he, too, wrestled with secularization and the alleged "death of God." In *The Land of Ulro* (1977), he whimsically captured the human consequences of our dual loss of faith in God and Reason: modern man finds himself with only "the starry sky above, and no moral law within." We are a long way from Kant's rational faith in "practical reason."

For his part, the great Russian writer Aleksandr Solzhenitsyn thought that the disasters of the twentieth century happened because "men have forgotten God," a forgetting that also entailed loss of confidence in the reality of the human soul where good and evil, and an enduring moral order, orient the choices of men (see Solzhenitsyn's 1983 *Templeton Lecture*). Miłosz and Solzhenitsyn self-consciously spoke the language of "good and evil," truth and liberty. Both spoke of the soul and responsibility before a God who is a friend to all. In their poems, essays, novels, and writings, they did not so much "re-enchant" the world as give us access to a moral order, an order of things, that a rationality worthy of the name must ultimately account for. Their spiritual and philosophical discernment, confronting evil in the form of twentieth-century totalitarianism, reminds us of the terrible self-limitation of modern reason. A reason that cannot speak about the drama of good and evil in the human soul, that cannot see totalitarian mendacity for what it is, that cannot call tyranny by its name, cannot apprehend the human world for what it is. As Leo Strauss argued in *On Tyranny*, it is not truly "scientific." As the phenomenologists would say, it cannot "save the appearances." The positivistic self-limitation of reason cuts us off from reason's "true greatness," as Pope Benedict XVI strikingly put it, and leaves us vulnerable to the contemporary "dictatorship of relativism." We are left with a radical divorce between truth and liberty, authority and subjectivity, one that leaves us to choose helplessly between secular fanaticism, religious fundamentalism, and democratic indifference.

Pope emeritus Benedict XVI, an eloquent partisan of both reason and faith, has sketched a better way in a series of writings and speeches over the last 25 years. With his help, I will show that Arnold's withdrawal of faith ultimately has its source in a crisis of reason, a reason that has limited itself, with grave consequences, to a narrow and soulless instrumental rationality.

Pope Benedict is the enemy of every kind of fideism. A faith worthy of the name affirms the liberating *Logos,* or Creative Reason, at the heart of the universe (this is one of Benedict's central theological ideas). The Christian God is not an oriental despot, a voluntaristic potentate whose will alone defines what is right and wrong. Christianity itself does not eschew philosophical inquiry or in any way endorse irrationality. Like his predecessor Pope John Paul II, Benedict believes that there is something "providential" in the encounter between Greek philosophy and biblical religion (see John Paul II's *Fides et Ratio*). Christians are obliged to give a rational account of their faith—apologetics are never reducible to propaganda (on this, Benedict appeals to 1 *Peter* 3:15). In his 2006 Regensburg address, Benedict laments the "dehellenization" of Christianity—its reduction to a humanitarian religion closed off to a rational articulation of nature and reason. Christianity is nothing if it is merely a "humanitarian moral message," an invitation to this-worldly amelioration or revolutionary transformation. Nor is it separable from the "natural moral law" available to reason and conscience. With the help of Pope Benedict's wonderfully thoughtful and suggestive address to the German parliament, or Bundestag, on September 22, 2011, I will trace the ways one might begin to overcome the fatal "self-limitation" of modern reason and the "dictatorship of relativism" that accompanies it.

In the Bundestag address, Pope Benedict speaks both as a German patriot and as the bishop of Rome. His subject is simultaneously moral and political: "the foundations of a free state of law (*Recht*)." His starting point is practical, since every statesman and citizen must wrestle with what it means to act in a just and lawful manner. He begins his reflection with a brief story from sacred scripture. Let us quote the text at some length:

> In the First Book of Kings, it is recounted that God invited the young King
> Solomon, on his accession to the throne, to make a request. What will the
> young ruler ask for at this important moment? Success—wealth—long
> life—destruction of his enemies? He chooses none of these things. Instead
> he asks for a "listening heart" so that he may govern God's people, and
> discern between good and evil. (cf. 1 *Kings* 3:9)

A "listening heart" is a cognitive and moral faculty—it is not a mere source of feelings and intuitions. It is more than a "discerning mind," as some versions of the Bible problematically translate this passage. A listening heart gives us access to an objective moral order that transcends mere subjectivity. It is a beautiful poetic rendering of what the tradition means by conscience. Conscience is that indispensable vehicle for connecting our liberty and judgment with truth and reason. Choice is never merely arbitrary, bereft of rational moral guidance. Without the access that conscience gives us to truth and justice, power becomes an instrument "for destroying right," at best Augustine's "great band of robbers" and, at worst, the open nihilism of the totalitarians who in the 1930s and 1940s drove Germany and the "whole world" to "the edge of the abyss."

The twentieth century's experience with Communist and National Socialist totalitarianism reminds us of what happens when we reject the primacy of conscience. The causes of the totalitarian episode were not some intellectual "monism" or "totalizing truth," as our relativists and postmoderns like to claim. This is the weakness of the liberalism of an Isaiah Berlin, one that constantly invokes pluralism but is afraid to appeal to truth in the most capacious sense of the term. Rather, the destruction of the listening heart, the civilizing traditions and memories to which it appealed, and the denial of the availability of right and wrong to objective reason all paved the way for the totalitarian negation of Western civilization. The totalitarian lie radicalized the subjectivism and relativism at the heart of liberal modernity. It did not so much re-enchant the world as empty it of all the resources of faith and reason. Comprehensive relativism, the denial of God and a natural order of things, and not some alleged moral absolutism, is at the source of the worst tragedies of the twentieth century. Pope Benedict never speaks in the name of "moral absolutism." Rather, he points to the humanizing discernment made possible by conscience.

I have already noted that Pope Benedict is a foe of every form of fideism and religious fanaticism. Like St. Paul in the *Epistle to the Romans*, he appeals to the law that "is written on men's hearts," a law to which the conscience "bears witness" (*Romans* 2:14 f.). As Benedict says in the Bundestag address, Christianity does not propose "a revealed law to the State and society." It respects the integrity of the political sphere and does not ask for revealed truth to become the explicit foundation of secular law. It does not completely conflate—or separate—the "things of God" and the "things of Caesar." Rather, with the Stoics, "it has pointed to nature and reason as the true sources of law," nature and reason mediated by our "listening hearts." Pope Benedict does not claim that the German Basic Law of 1949 (or other modern affirmations of human rights) owes everything to Christianity, but he does not understand how its claims made on behalf of human liberty and dignity can be justified without "Solomon's listening heart, a reason that is open to the language of being." That phrase beautifully articulates the difference between classical Christian reason and the positivist substitute for it.

The dogmatic separation of the "is" and the "ought" at the heart of modern philosophical discussions of ethics make nature simply functional, devoid of guidance for ethics and politics. It is an impersonal system of cause and effect with no relevance for ethics or common life. Norms are said to be rooted in will and thus pure arbitrariness (see Hans Kelsen, who is referred to by Pope Benedict in the Bundestag address), and not reason and truth. Benedict protests against this reduction of ethics to the realm of will and subjectivity. He insists that there is an "ecology of man" that must be acknowledged by all those who care for truth and human dignity. "Man too has a nature that he must respect and that he cannot manipulate at will." Contemporary Europeans have become ardent ecologists, as the pope appreciatively notes; at the same time, they increasingly repudiate the natural moral limits inherent in the human condition. Crucially, Benedict adds that "Man is not merely self-creating freedom," as the existentialists would claim. Benedict draws all the necessary conclusions for a true moral ecology of human freedom and responsibility. Man "is intellect and will, but he is also nature, and his will is rightly ordered if he respects his nature, listens to it and accepts himself for who he is, as one who did not create himself." The beginning of wisdom is to know men are not gods. The Pope insists: "In this way, and in no other, is true human freedom fulfilled." Benedict's quarrel is not with democracy per se, but with its jettisoning of the ecology of freedom, rooted in conscience and "the listening heart," that gives ample moral content to our freedom.

In discussing the true foundations of law, Benedict returns us to the Old West of Jerusalem, Athens, and Rome. This return is not carried out for the sake of rejecting modern liberty, but to reveal its salutary dialectical dependence on "Israel's monotheism, the philosophical reason of the Greeks and Roman Law." Europe did not begin with the Enlightenment, not to mention May 1968 (the starting point of what we can call "humanitarian" or "post-Western" democracy). The "inviolable dignity of every single person" and the true criteria of law stand or fall with our recognition of the guiding light that is the "listening heart," that moral and cognitive faculty that gives us "the capacity to discern between good and evil, and thus to establish true law, to serve justice and peace."

As Benedict's 1992 essay "Conscience and Truth" makes clear, Benedict sides with Cardinal Newman in rejecting any identification of conscience with subjectivism and relativism. The redoubtable Catholic convert deferred to conscience in all things, and saw in it the indispensable cornerstone of the Catholic faith. As Benedict writes, for Newman and the tradition on which he draws "conscience means the abolition of mere subjectivity when man's intimate sphere is touched by the truth that comes from God." A "true man of conscience," such as St. Thomas More, "did not in the least regard conscience as the expression of his subjective tenacity or of an eccentric heroism." Conscience is our portal to the natural moral law, and it is indeed written "in the hearts of men." Subjective tenacity is what the Hungarian philosopher Aurel Kolnai called a "second-level good." As such, it can be compatible with evil as well as good (the same can be said for the "authenticity" so valued by modern relativists).

Benedict also clarifies the Church's teaching on our obligation to obey even an "erring conscience." Conscience entails a "primal remembrance of the good and true," an *anamnesis* that the Church and our civilized inheritance reinforces and sustains. Ideological fanatics such as Hitler and Stalin who arrive at "perverse convictions" do so by "trampling down the protest made by the anamnesis of one's true being." Dulled to truth by ideological lies, they are guilty at a much deeper ontological level. Their perverse convictions are wholly separated from conscience, rightly understood.

Pope Benedict's discussion of conscience and "the listening heart" is just one way in which his thought and work enlarges reason and reveals its "true greatness." His reflections, at once theoretical and practical, theological and moral-political, can be fruitfully compared to the complementary witness of the anti-totalitarian dissidents of the East. Solzhenitsyn's appeal to "live not by lies!" (and his concomitant insistence that "the line dividing good and evil cuts through the heart of every human being") and Václav Havel's reflections on "politics and conscience" point in the same broad direction. Solzhenitsyn's and Havel's admirable defiance of the Communist behemoth was inseparably a call for "living in truth." That call did not cease to be relevant after the fall of European totalitarianism. Only by reconnecting truth and liberty, politics and conscience, can modern man free himself from what C. S. Lewis called "the poison of subjectivism." By pursuing such a reconnection, we might take some sure-footed steps toward delivering on the promise of a liberty worthy of man. In doing so, we can begin to repel the humanitarian subversion of Christianity—and of authentic political life.

• SOURCES AND SUGGESTED READINGS •

I have drawn on the speeches in *Liberating Logos: Pope Benedict XVI's September Speeches*, edited by Marc D. Guerra, Preface by James V. Schall (South Bend, IN: St. Augustine's Press, 2014). I am indebted to Marc D. Guerra's "Preface" for its emphasis on the theme of the excessive "self-limitation of modern reason" in Pope Benedict's thought. The Bundestag address of September 22, 2011, can be found on pp. 39–48.

Pope Benedict's superb 1992 reflection on "Conscience and Truth" can be found in Pope Benedict XVI, *Values in a Time of Upheaval* (New York: Crossroad Publishing, 2006), pp. 75–97. See the luminous discussion of Newman and Socrates as "Signposts to Conscience" on pp. 84–90.

The Humanitarian versus the Religious Attitude[1]

Aurel Kolnai (1944)

I

A completely or an originally irreligious civilization has in all likelihood never existed, but it is not, in itself, unimaginable; what is more important, the modern civilization of Western mankind, originally (and still, in part, actually) Christian, has revealed a trend of evolution towards a society in which, practically speaking, religion as a determining factor of private and public life is to yield its place to a nonreligious, immanentistic, secular moral orientation which may best be described succinctly as "humanitarian." While such a prospect cannot but appall the believer, it has also evoked misgivings and apprehension in a good many nonreligious or not emphatically religious students of human civilization; nay, terrified some of them, perhaps, to an extent to which it could never terrify the believer himself. For it is precisely the nobler and more perspicacious kind of mundane thinker who is apt to be worried primarily about the fate of human civilization as such, than which he knows no higher thing. Yet it is a grave problem, and one that poses itself on a purely worldly level of thinking, how far an irreligious civilization can subsist at all, or how soon it is bound to degenerate into a state of barbarism: in other words, whether humanitarianism is essentially capable of maintaining itself in actual reality or is fated to defeat its own ends, thus marking but a brief transition towards disintegration and anarchy—coupled, of necessity, with new phenomena of tyranny and new forms of gross and superstitious creeds widely dissimilar

---

1 This essay, which originally appeared in *The Thomist* in 1944, is republished with the permission of John Haldane (St. Andrew's University), Aurel Kolnai's literary executor.

to its own mental world. It goes without saying that the rise of Communism and of Fascism—most characteristically, however, of Nazism—is entirely calculated to impress the observer as premonitory signs (if not more) of just such a turn of evolution.

The problem I have indicated concerns the Catholic less directly and from a somewhat different angle, but concern him it certainly does. It is not only that we are interested in civilization as against barbarity; nor, merely, the greater freedom the Church may hope to enjoy under a tolerant humanitarian system as compared with fresh brands of virulent paganism and a totalitarian idolatry of secular power; it is also well for us to understand wholly and in all its implications the *intrinsic* inadequacy of humanitarianism, so as to be able to help our non-Catholic and non-Christian fellows towards a fuller understanding thereof. For secular preoccupations of a legitimate and dignified kind have often in history supplied valuable and important elements of society with the initial motives for their conversions to the Faith.

The sketchy remarks which follow, destined to throw some light on a very few aspects of the vast problem, are purely analytic in character, and in no way supposed to contribute directly to a historic prognosis or a cultural program. I may also observe that I intend to examine, here, the "humanitarian" attitude as contrasted to the "religious" attitude in general, rather than to the specifically Catholic one. By no means does this imply, however, any leaning towards the shallow and absurd view that all religions "teach essentially the same thing"; nor indeed the view that any kind of "religiousness" is necessarily better, or more consonant with the basic values of Civilization, than the irreligious attitude in its humanitarian form.

II

A few clarifications regarding nomenclature may seem advisable.

1. By a "religious attitude" we mean a corporate—or at least, a socially relevant—outlook on human affairs which contains a reference to a "higher" Power (or a system of such powers) underlying "cosmic" reality, and invested with a "claim" to determine, direct, or guide human thought and behavior. The term "higher" is meant to indicate an order of Reality qualitatively distinct from the natural order of things and events as experienced in the everyday existence of a given society, including even such unknown objects

and forces as can at any rate be imagined as mere additional elements essentially fitting into the texture of natural reality. The word "higher" (for which "transcendent," or, in a looser sense, "supernatural" may be substituted) also connotes a specific relationship between the supposed Power and the gradation of recognized values, as well as the hierarchy of social dignities, within natural reality itself: deities are usually, though in various manners and degrees, conceived as the sources, guardians and guarantors of law and morality; as paragons and measures of holiness and rectitude; moreover, as exemplars and incarnations of things noble and things royal. The "Power" in question is also credited with a specific relation to "cosmic" reality: with a faculty of creative and ordering activity, in regard to the things of nature, on a radically and incomparably vaster scale than the human one; a tendency towards assumptions of universality, omnipotence, and creativeness proper is mostly present in some form.

Thus, in religion, the incommensurableness between man and the cosmic forces which surround and condition him without, apparently, being affected by his actions in any but an infinitesimal sense, is at the same time reaffirmed and—tentatively, at least—healed: man is no longer simply a hopeless exile lost in the vastness of things extra-human of which he is doomed to occupy a tiny corner; by dint of his proper contact with the Divine, to which cosmic reality is subject or in which it is centered, he comes to fill a rightful place, to assume a positional value as it were, in the Universe (whatever his concrete conception of the latter). Finally, to the Divine—though its personal nature be represented in a vague and uncertain fashion only—is attributed a "claim" on man; in other words, man's cognition of the Divine inherently entails obligations on his part. These are always closely interrelated, though never purely and simply identical, with whatever he experiences as moral obligations. The duties and functions of men (in society, or under the eyes of society) thus appear to be specifically incorporated in the ultimate principles of Being as such. I have, naturally, employed a more or less modern and technical language (though, as best I could, a "neutral" one), rather unlike the terms in which actual religious consciousness is wont to express itself; yet it is in some such way, I think, that the main purport of that consciousness may be conceptually grasped.

It remains to be added, however, that the religious attitude also very generally encloses what we might briefly call a negativistic aspect: a tendency to break, to pierce—at least, to modify and to relativize—man's natural egoism, lust, and joy of life. The motifs of asceticism, sacrifice, self-renunciation, of fear and awe tinging the reverence due to the assumed higher powers, are by no means confined to Hinduism and Christianity; in some form or other, they reappear in practically every religion. Some consciousness (be it ever so dim and rudimentary) of the Fall and of the corruption of human nature, of the need to "propitiate" the "angry" or "jealous" godhead—or again, of man's need to "purify" himself by techniques mostly involving asceticism—are seldom absent. It is by making him aware of his ambiguous and precarious status as a natural being that religion provides man with a more settled and enhanced position in the face of cosmic nature. His impotence in relation to his environment is rendered more bearable, and indeed even actually lessened in various indirect ways: but this is granted at the price only that he refrains from certain actions which he *could* perform without even becoming liable to any immediate or clearly consecutive punishment, and that he constrains himself to certain other actions which by themselves are entirely strange, and even contrary, to the trend of his primary and "normal" needs.

In connection therewith, the religious attitude always fastens on some element of mystery, too; some concrete and particular myths, holy objects, rituals and rules of conduct: things which from the very outset (and not only in our modern consciousness) essentially differ from the "evident" and more generally communicable data of both experimental world-interpretation and rational morality. In all religion there is some aspect of the mysterious and arbitrary, distinct from normal everyday orientation: something that—apart, perhaps, from such rather specific states of mind as are described under the name of "primitive" animism—subsists as an alien body in the midst of the otherwise prevailing types of thought and "pattern of reactions." The religious contact is definitely experienced as an "irruption" into the natural set of relationships. (Thus the belief in miracles does not, as the pitiably shallow philosophy of enlightenment would have it, issue from ignorance of the "laws of nature"; on the contrary, the very concept of the miraculous presupposes a familiarity with the laws of nature.)

Finally, I have alluded to the "corporate" character, if not of all religious belief or experience as such, yet of all religious systems and practices. Religion is essentially not a matter of "opinions," "convictions," or "conscience," though these may play a legitimate part in a man's basic acceptance or rejection of a religion, and again in their turn are conditioned by one's religious allegiance and outlook. In fact, religion always intrinsically tends to be "tribal" or "national," or again, whether or not with a universalistic intent, to constitute a community of its own—a "church." And, unlike many other types of "association," the community coordinated to a religion tends to enter into the thematic content of that religion: the ruler is a descendant or a member of divinity; the people is a chosen or a priestly one; the Church herself, as a body, is holy. The adherents of a religion experience it, not only as important and as uniting, but as the token, and the generative principle as it were, of a specification of mankind aware of its own identity. If the religion is frankly universalistic, as is the case with Christianity, then mankind as a whole is deemed to be destined to reshape itself in the concrete community of the "children of God."

2. The irreligious attitude, on the other side, need not of course be what we call a "humanitarian" one. An un-spiritual, purely private and "selfish" outlook on life, for instance, is of fairly common occurrence even in religious ages. Humanitarianism, however, is the standard type of non-religious philosophy. It has risen, in unprecedented vigor, on a soil tilled by Christianity: that is to say, in our own modern age characterized by a decaying and shrinking Christian religiousness. Obviously, Christianity at a stage of disintegration and retreat is calculated to prepare the ground for humanitarianism, for the Christian religion itself, being universalistic, personalistic and moralistic, we may even say in a sense rationalistic, bears a strong connotation of humanitarianism in the broader sense of the term. It places man as such in the center of the created universe; hence the Christian in the process of losing hold of his religion, and restricting his interests to the world of creaturely things, is likely to set up "man as such" as the measure of everything, and to develop a humanitarian outlook. Many simple minds among the modern half-educated hold that humanitarianism is all that is essential and worthy of respect in Christianity: he who devotes his cares to "social welfare" is the "true Christian," though he may not believe in the biblical God, that "old gentleman with a big white beard,"—seeing that he obeys conscientiously the injunctions of Jesus the great "teacher" of "unselfishness." Many moderns less naive, and some of them actually Christians, maintain that humanitarianism is nothing but "Christianity rationalized," which in their eyes may mean either a "perfected" or an impoverished Christianity. The truth is that humanitarianism is one of the primary, inherent possibilities of our philosophical orientation; it is

revealed, for example, in certain types of ancient thought represented by men who lived long before the Incarnation and never heard or cared about the Jewish God. But certainly modern liberal society, with its mental complexion mixed of Christian, semi-Christian and post-Christian ingredients, exhibits the traits of humanitarianism with a unique sharpness and completeness.

The humanitarian attitude, then, takes its departure from the "human needs" in a comprehensive sense of the word: what "men" desire and what they fear, what "men" appreciate and what they loathe, what promises to secure or to enhance and what is apt to threaten or to stunt the "development" and the "happiness" of "men" is to provide us with the basic data for our orientation. All kinds of "needs" and the "needs" of all men or groups of men are equally legitimate in principle; any preconceived bias or restriction is illegitimate. Account is to be taken, indeed, of the mutual interdependence and conditioning of the "needs," including the tensions and antagonistic relations among them: hence the necessity for a (temporary) repression of needs, and for their "scaling" as well as for their "education," is granted. But certainly human needs can only be opposed by—or, on the strength of—more imperious and urgent, more general and more durable needs. We must have a selective recognition and rejection or postponement of needs: but this must be effected on the basis of a purely immanent consideration of the needs themselves—that is, on a basis of "reason"; it must not be done in deference to any prejudice claiming absolute recognition over and above human needs as such—which would mean "superstition" in the place of reason.

A strictly humanitarian orientation is, of course, impossible in practice, because an all-embracing conspectus of mankind's needs is beyond the mental range of its members, taken individually and collectively; "arbitrary preferences" of various kinds will always enter, though sometimes surreptitiously; they tend to change more or less rapidly in the typical humanitarian mentality, which logically involves a cult of flexibility and adaptability. As regards the metaphysical interpretation of the world most suited to humanitarian ethics, it is inherent in the creed itself that this cannot be more than a secondary concern; on the whole, however, some variety of a naturalistic, mechanistic and sensualistic pattern is undoubtedly preferable, since an attempt to "explain" the world with the exclusion of "transcendent" entities is best in tune with the central tenet: the immanent sovereignty of human needs. Yet a deistic, pantheistic, or even "Christian," phrase-ology may seem quite permissible: for a really consistent, broadminded humanitarianism will not hesitate to register the "religious needs of man," as well as his "aesthetic needs," along with the more serious ones. In any concrete question of morals, moreover, humanitarianism may (and often does) happen to arrive at the same conclusion as, say, Catholicism. That the irreligious-humanitarian morality is in no case actually and intrinsically "the same" as any religious morality, and in what typical ways it tends to differ therefrom in a material and tangible sense, will be examined in the third and main part of this article.

3. Before that, however, we must devote some attention to the phenom-enon of quasi-religious attitudes. Man does indeed stand in great "need" of religion: wherefore, whenever the traditional religion of a civilization is weakening, and irreligious patterns of thought acquire ascendency in men's minds, a secondary appearance of semi-religious or para-religious attitudes can be observed. We are faced with a heretical watering-down of the traditional religion, arbitrary qualifications of the humanitarian creed, semi-scientific fads and fashions, autochthonous or imported superstitions actually believed or flaunted as a matter of diversion, political ideologies assuming a religious tinge and fervor, and the like.

In our own days, Communism and Nazism are sometimes described as "pseudo-religions"; the label is erroneous, particularly in the case of Communism, for what is present there is not so much worldly incentives operating under a pretense of religion as an attitude akin to the religious one which is camouflaged as a "scientific" or purely political doctrine. Hence we ought rather to speak of "crypto-religion," or use the standard term adopted by some critics of totalitarianism: "secular religion." In fact, concepts purely immanent, natural and scientific in appearance, such as the "dialectic evolution of productive forces" or the "world revolution," the "Nordic race" or the "Germanic values" etc., come to assume a psy-chological function not devoid of certain "religious" traits; for not only do they claim devotion and self-sacrifice, they also carry with them a note of mystery and arbitrary specification, they seem to embody a self-subsistent reality "transcendent" to the rational operations of the individual mind, and, in a word, they belong to the realm not merely of political ideology but of "collective myths." Lenin and Stalin, and Hitler to an even higher degree, unmistakably represent mythical figures in a far more proper and pretentious sense of the term than do the liberal, revolutionary and nationalist political heroes of the last hundred and fifty years, or the minor dictators of our own days.

In a very loose way of speech, we might of course call the ideology of the French Revolution a "religious" one, as it is certainly anything but a plain statement of "scientific truth"; but much more properly may we so describe Communism, and again in a yet stricter sense, Nazi racialism. Although, in fact, the "self-evident truths" of the liberal revolutionary ideology are far less "self-evident" than they were made out to be, and may in part be no truths at all, they are *conceived as* "self-evident" to anybody's individual reason as such; their *appeal* is directed simply to the "enlightened self-interest" of men. The aspect of "revelation" and "prophethood" implied in Marxism-Leninism, and in a franker fashion and with stronger metaphysical connotations, in Hitlerism, has no counterpart at all in the sphere of humanitarian liberalism. Nor do I think we are justified in calling nationalism the "religion of the present age." A virulent and operative creed, enclosing even a good deal of unreasonableness, need not be anything like a religion: the latter requires an element of cosmic reference, of superhuman afflatus, of mystical transcendency, experienced—though not perhaps formulated—as such.

A society absolutely addicted to humanitarian irreligion seems well-nigh impossible; the predominance of this creed will be mitigated by various "substitutes for religion" which in a religious society would not be present or would be present in a less emphatic, a more simply natural form only. Besides, in the humanitarian societies we know Christianity itself has survived, though largely in a fragmentary shape, and in a restricted and equivocal position. But Communism and especially Nazism, signalizing the advance in depth of the crisis, seem to announce the possible advent of genuine new religions opposed to humanitarianism. This, however, is not meant as a prognosis. It is conceivable that all attempts to introduce new heathen religions in a society impregnated with Christianity will prove abortive; that there will follow a reviviscence of the old religion, or again, a consolidation and expansion of the humanitarian system made more livable, for some time, by subordinate religious factors like traditional Christianity, a somewhat tamed Communism, and possibly others to come.

To avoid a crude misconception, it may be worth noting that "genuine religion" has nothing, of course, to do with "true religion" or "authentic faith." "Genuine religion" belongs to a purely natural, socio-psychological, descriptive order of concepts; it is quite irrespective of the truth or untruth of the given religion's claim and contents. Several religions may not be essentially true at the same time, nor even enclose the same amount of partial truth; but many contradictory religions may well be fully "genuine religions" at the same time. The worshippers of Baal professed a more genuine religion than many present adherents of a vague and threadbare Christianity soaked in humanitarianism; yet there is more truth, according to our belief, in the religious "persuasions" of the latter than in those of the idolaters.

III

Turning, now, to the differential description of the humanitarian as contrasted to the religious attitude, we must naturally qualify our query. That the religious mind places God, or the Deity, or things divine, in the center of its outlook upon life, whereas irreligious humanitarianism does not admit of these except perhaps as mere verbal decorations—this is not the difference which interests us here but only the premise to it: the definition underlying the question. We might best put the actual question in the form of an initial doubt on its relevancy. There is an obvious nexus between religion and morality; but most of us have known definitely moral men who were wholly, or all but, irreligious. Civilizations seem to be called into life, and sustained, by religions; but, to put it in guarded terms, a case can be made out for progresses being possible in a civilization weakening in religion and approaching the creed of irreligious humanitarianism.

We may prefer, and prefer infinitely (supposing, in particular, that we are already believers in one given religion) religion plus morality, and religion plus civilization, to morality and civilization alone; or again, to express it differently, morality or civilization inspired and informed by religion to morality or civilization built on irreligious foundations. Yet at the same time we might be obliged to admit that *as* morality or civilization pure and simple, one may look very much like the other. To take one very plain example: I may, at the risk of my own life, rescue a fellow-man from a burning house, because I obey God's commandment enjoining the love of one's neighbor; but I may equally do so without believing in any divine legislation, because I consider it a moral duty on humanitarian grounds. It would be a false notion (and, let it be stressed particularly, by no means a Catholic one) that in the second case my action, though objectively useful, cannot be a genuinely moral one. Certainly I may also rescue the man from danger because he is a debtor of mine, or in order to boast of my courage; but that is not the supposition. On the other hand, quasi-religious motives may also sometimes approximate towards a crude utilitarianism in reference to expectations in the hereafter.

Not only is it possible for a man to understand, to appreciate, and to cultivate, say, justice, kindness and self-control, without referring them back to the qualities and the will of God, but (in orthodox Catholic doctrine at least) the immanent distinction of Good and Evil is one of the logical premises to the Faith itself (God is good, and wills the good; the good is *not* simply "what God wills"). Are we, then, concerned with a mere difference in the ultimate *motivation* of moral behavior, without any bearing on the *essential contents*, as well as the actual recognition, of morality?

1. It is indeed the problem of motivation, and, linked to that, the problem of obligation on which the defenders of religious morals have dwelt most insistently when criticizing humanitarian ethics. From recognizing the good to practicing it, from discerning moral values to accepting the sometimes very onerous obligations they entail, it is a far cry: religious belief in a cosmic reality specifically related to the moral law, and it alone, will guarantee the acceptation of that sacrifice, the translation of moral cognition and preference into terms of action—with the renunciation of pleasures and the endurance of hardships implicit therein. The irreligious man may fulfill his duties so long as they are pleasant; he may also comply with unpleasant ones so long as the privation of satisfactions they involve is moderate, and there is a recompense in sight on another level of pleasures; but as soon as duty pure and simple confronts the behest of the senses or the possessive instinct, duty will prove weaker: as soon as the man's morality is put to the ultimate and decisive test, it will break down. Viewed in the average perspective, this argument is certainly sound; though it is worth remembering that moral life as a whole does not predominantly consist of "ultimate and decisive tests" and heroic situations, and that religious moralists and pedagogues, too, are almost invariably eager to point out the physical and secular usefulness of a moral conduct and the probable deleterious consequences of sin.

It is more important for us to emphasize, however, that irreligion is also bound to impair moral *cognition* itself. True, the irreligious mind may discern good from evil; but again it may not. Whereas our primary "moral sense" as such does not depend on religious concepts, it yields no concrete, certain, and fully articulated knowledge of good and evil: the latter requires an authoritative divine guidance (which may reach us either in an authentically revealed or, at any rate, in a vague, dimmed, and partly distorted form). Whenever, on the other hand, a moral duty strikes the "decent" but irreligious man as definitely unpleasant, he may well tend to explain it away and to develop a falsified ethic in order to escape both material unpleasantness and the equally unpleasant consciousness of moral guilt or inferiority. Against such an aberration he is protected by no sure safeguard. The humanitarian ethicist who takes his stand on the comprehensive system of "human needs" will no doubt arrive at many materially correct conclusions: first, because true morality in fact closely corresponds with the universal and perennial "needs of man," and secondly, because our supposed ethicist, if he is intelligent, will take account of the "data" of the natural "moral sense," too (that is, of men's average moral preferences and judgments), in his calculus of "human needs"; yet nothing need keep him from placing, in regard to certain problems and in given cases, the urge of morally indifferent or intrinsically reprehensible "needs" (which he deems to be more pressing, more general, or more unalterable) above even very clearly voiced imperatives of the "moral sense." Not only, then, is irreligious morality a fragile thing in practice, but humanitarian ethic, too, is at its best a flimsy texture at the mercy of *inherent* dangers.

Moreover, it must be axiomatic even for the non-religious but unprejudiced student that humanitarian and religious morality must *always* be different in *quality*. I am not hinting, of course, at the "supernatural virtues" treated in Catholic philosophy, which logically presuppose the belief in transcendent objects of veneration, but am entirely confining myself to the sphere of natural morality. The moral judgment (the act of approval or disapproval as such), the moral decision and outward action, may occasionally or frequently be the same; the moral experience as a whole—even in reference to limited cases or subject-matters—is never the same. For the religious consciousness will, whenever a "moral attitude" is elicited, experience the divine exemplar, codifier and guarantor of virtue at least as a background element of the situation. God is, generally speaking, not the thematic center of natural morality, but the underlying relationship with Him cannot but color and complete even the humblest moral act of deliberation or decision, however humdrum its object. We may understand the "nerve" of justice, as it were (and behave accordingly), without any reference to divine justice ordering the world and providing even human justice with a supreme sanction; but with such a reference wanting or being excluded, we are cut off from the full meaning of justice—applied to matters howsoever trifling.

On the impossible supposition that there were no God, I should still speak "the truth" in affirming that a cardboard box now lying on my writing-desk is yellow and circular, and tell a "falsehood" in asserting that it is blue and hexagonal; yet the thought of God having revealed Truth and not falsehood, of Jesus having risen from the dead "in truth" (which the suspicious and critical Thomas quite understandably doubted at first but was ultimately compelled to admit on the strength of a supremely realistic test), of "*Ego sum via*, veritas *et vita*," of true dogma and false heresy, etc., provides Truth, if I may so put it, with a sounding-board of sacredness and inexorable earnestness, should the "truth" in question even concern the color and shape of an unimportant object. Apart from the cases of sensual attraction, particular personal "fancying," or unpersonal tribal "identification," the love of our fellow-men will bear a prim, ice-cold, mutilated quality unless it be grounded in the love of Him Who alone is absolutely worthy of love and Who bestows His gratuitous primal love upon all of us. Humility and reverence in the human relationships which properly require them may be possible without religious piety, but they cannot help losing depth, savor, and firmness, if the sphere of their primary and standard objects is removed.

The realm of "*mores*" (that is, of morally relevant social custom) is perhaps even more intimately dependent on religious allegiance than the realm of morality proper. It is by no means in Christian communities alone that *asebeia* has been felt to be inseparable from anarchy and moral disintegration. The reconciliation of personal freedom, dignity, selfhood, and vitality with the requirements of social discipline and coordination, though it may be conceived on extra-religious grounds, constitutes a special function of religion (owing to the specifically "uniting" power of religious experience, and for other reasons which cannot be discussed here); in this matter, particularly, the humanitarian experiment is drawing on the dwindling resources of Christianity, and the precarious balance it has achieved exhibits the signs of shifting towards a totalitarian or "identitarian" loss of liberty and personality: a self-idolatry of "society" pregnant, perhaps, with new types of pagan quasi-religiousness.

2. In sum, the primordial contrast between religious and humanitarian morality lies in the metaphysical substructure, and accordingly, in the ultimate or "official" *motivation* rather than in the contents; but motivation and contents are far from being radically separable from each other, and, though it be in variable ways and degrees, an essentially altered motivation is certain to react upon the contents themselves. Thus, generally speaking, irreligious humanitarianism necessarily involves a certain bias for immoralism inasmuch as it has no room for the concept of intrinsic moral evil, and of the moral scissure in human nature. Rejecting all intrinsic discrimination between human "needs," and interpreting moral "evil" merely in terms of impulses which in given conditions are likely to interfere with the fulfillment of more imperious, general, and permanent "needs," it is bound to profess an ethical "positivism" cleared from all experience of "sin," which is tantamount to a flattening out of all moral life into a technique of the gratification of desires. True, the full substantiality or self-subsistence of "evil" is questioned in certain religious systems of thought, too (thus, in Catholicism as against Manichaeism); but not withstanding the essential goodness of being as such, at least in a secondary sense the existence of intrinsic evil—of a basic perversion of the will—is not only admitted but centrally emphasized. Hence, a tendency in favor of the "free will," of responsibility in the strict sense, of a fundamental distinction between formal and merely material defects of human conduct, and of the idea of retaliation: a tendency entirely alien to the humanitarian attitude.

The humanitarian attitude will lean towards making the goodness or badness of any type of conduct dependent on the part it may play in a functional framework of situations; placing instincts and moods on a footing with the direction of the will, manifestations of the "subconscious" with decisions enacted by man's central personality, deficiency in "training" or "development" as well as "disease" with malice and deliberate wickedness; and substituting "cure" or "prevention," "education" or "elimination," for all retaliation proper. To the humanitarian mind, Raskolnikov's "claim" to slaying and despoiling the old usurer will probably appear "erroneous," but not altogether absurd (on the one hand, the old woman's "right to live" is as much a primary "datum" as everybody else's; on the other, a strong and gifted young man represents a so much greater volume of "needs" and so much more potential usefulness for "society" that his "miscalculation" is at any rate understandable); while the public authority's right to execute the murderer must obviously appear absurd and fictitious—for the infliction of death and suffering will not be made undone but merely aggravated by the consequent infliction of more death and suffering. Under humanitarianism, the judgment of crime will tend to degenerate into a mere protection of "majority" interests: to shrink to a mere repression of the inconvenient—or again, perhaps, to expand into a suppression of whatever may be deemed inconvenient. The selfsame mentality that rejects the concept of punishing the evildoer as "superstitious" or a "mere disguise for the primitive urge of revenge" may glibly accept the "elimination" of the "unfit for life" or the "maladjusted" as an act of "higher humanity."

3. It can be maintained that, in spite of its essential bent towards immoralism, the humanitarian attitude may also at certain phases find expression in a kind of hyper-moralism. Such transitional phases in the process of the impoverishment and evaporation of corporate religion have been marked, for instance, by waves of hyper-moralism of the Stoic and the Puritan type. An intensified, systematized and particularized moral strain may be substituted for the vanishing mystical substance of religion; with faith proper growing more doubtful, reduced and threadbare, a crampedly "impeccable" life may serve to demonstrate one's "effective" belief in whatever is "truly essential" in religion, or one's actual membership in the body of the "elect" or the "wise."

In advanced humanitarianism, the aspect of hyper-moralism will still be present but bear a different tinge. It will no longer cling to arbitrary relics from the old religious morality (including this or that element of material, "mystical" ethics, as well as the overstressing of individual "conscience") but appear more strictly formalistic and organizational: while morality no longer consists in anything but a rational and comprehensive administration of "human needs" as such, men's vision is directed to *ensuring* a "moral world" and an omnipresence of moral conduct. There is not much sense left in the concept of sexual purity; but, on the other hand, a large-scale building of spacious apartments for everybody will cause sexual impurity to disappear automatically and universally. The "solution of the economic problem" will similarly do away with hatred, jealousy, greed, petty egoism, etc., for when all will live in abundance, there will be no need for anybody to develop such emotions. Liquor prohibition, the outlawry of war, the organized World State, universal free trade, institutionalized national self-determination, etc., come within the same context. Certainly moral values taken in any specific sense of the term seem to be engulfed and transposed here entirely in concepts of material or "psychic" welfare; but the less content attaches to the idea of moral perfection and the less moral substance appears to be left over, the more pretentious and cocksure becomes the pursuit of the claim to a formally "perfect" world, a morally "waterproof" and indeed a "foolproof" reality as it were.

4. In general, we may state that the humanitarian attitude, while not necessarily out of contact with moral as distinct from material or hedonic values, will be inclined to concentrate (more and more, in the progress of its unfolding) on *such* moral values as can be grasped somehow in analogy with the evidence of the outward senses. Hence the ascendancy a) of formalism, b) of materialism—as opposed a) to "material," "objective," or "intrinsic" value, b) to spiritual points of view. Supposing the primary sovereignty of human needs without any distinction derived from man's dependence on a higher sphere of being, and having regard to their most complex and variable interrelationship, our orientation will necessarily seek guidance from principles as "plain" and "neat" as possible, which are invested with a character of quasi-geometrical "self-evidence." The repression of inordinate self-seeking, the principle of commutative justice may carry as much appeal to the humanitarian as to the Christian; an appeal always lacking, of course, the complete weight of the Christian experience of good or ill, but occasionally, let it be admitted, exercising an even more acute and—transitorily, at least—more effective pressure. Every possibility of quantification will be seized upon: the "greatest good" of the "greatest number" is proclaimed; every inequality, at least every inequality not directly traceable to innate physiological differences, is frowned upon as an injustice. The differential characteristics of human persons will be negated unless they are verifiable by experimental and statistical methods. Much more attention is paid to the problem of making everyone alike share in the "good life" than to the query as to what the good life really is like; there is less and less care about the existence of standards of culture, but an enormous amount of thought and effort is devoted to the dissemination of culture through education; because the meaning and purpose of life are viewed as purely immanent, and therefore at once self-evident and insusceptible of definition, the technique of life

(with a particular stress on technology) becomes the object of a devotion unmistakably imbued with a kind of misplaced religious fervor.

The fatal tendency towards materialism is but another side to this. Taking needs as needs, the material needs of man are more massive, urgent and obtrusive than those of the soul, and therefore procure a surer guidance and a more fixed pattern of orientation. Everything else appears reduced to the status of a supplementary decoration; it is ordered on the model of the classic and proven organization of things material; the spiritual is tolerated or appreciated as an epiphenomenon, a superstructure, an article of luxury—gossamer stuff, as it were, that cannot be taken truly seriously in the face of the solid necessities and securities of the material sphere. Nor does this hang on the phrase "human needs," which I think is most expressive of the attitude in question, but is inherent in the very essence of that attitude; instead of "needs," we may as well choose as a dominant formula human "welfare" or "happiness," or even the "full unfolding of man's dispositions and capacities." All these may be, and very often are, interpreted generously and intelligently so as to comprise the spiritual, not excepting even the "religious yearning": yet, once the perspective of an imminent humanitarianism is adopted and maintained, the spiritual will be credited with no other mode of existence than a mere elongation or "sublimation" (that is, a possibly attractive but unnecessary and peripheric refinement) of the material, an affair of Sunday boredom or festive recreation, of after-dinner past-time or ungenuine romanticism.

An unprejudiced contemplation of "humanity," with its curious, manifold and contradictory attributes, is indeed calculated to draw us towards religion: in other words, towards the discovery of man's "fallenness" as well as his peculiar ontological nobility; of his relation to a supra-human reality which exists outside him; in a word, of the radical inadequacy of humanitarianism. However, given the premise of an artificial restriction to "humanity," implying the axiom that all "higher aspirations" of man are meaningless or at any rate irrelevant for us except *as* "higher aspirations of *man*"—irrespective of the objective goal towards which they point—the physical substratum of "human nature" cannot help occupying a central and overwhelming position. If a moribund patient is known to be a devout Catholic, or expresses the wish to receive the Sacraments, we will of course be considerate and complaisant enough to send for a priest, if only to apply a bit of soothing psychotherapy; but on the plane of terrestrial immanence, any drug which we hope to be ever so slightly efficacious will appear more important and needful than the religious ceremony.

"Culture," again, has no small prestige in the world of humanitarianism; but it has often been observed that it is valued in view of its being somehow translatable—through whatever more patent or more hidden channels of ideas, and interactions of forces—into terms of "money." The ultimately essential category is not, of course, "money" (it is not an affair of capitalism or market economy, with socialism as a "remedy"), but "welfare," economic security and super-security, protection and perfection of the functional mechanism of "life." "Culture" and its enjoyment is supposed to "educate," "recreate" and "ennoble" man: to render him fitter for work and more "productive," to alleviate the strains he must endure and to make him more amenable to smooth and rational "cooperation."

Anyhow, the claim of taking into account man's spiritual nature without a genuine and dominant reference to supra-human spiritual reality is comparable to pretending to a vision of man's physical nature without a knowledge of the lower animals and the realm of inanimate material things. In the climate of irreligion, man's spiritual functions and capacities (considered, even, in a purely natural context of objects), will—no matter how much lip-service and sincere enthusiasm be devoted to them—inevitably be under-stimulated, undernourished, under-exercised, and condemned to atrophy; it is the inherent nemesis of humanitarianism that the proclamation of man's "sovereignty" is bound to displace his center of gravity into the nether regions of his being, and to degrade his nature towards a level of sub-humanity. But, seeing that man is and remains man, he is certain to react, sooner or later, in a fashion unforeseen by his humanitarian shepherds: to react morbidly, dismally, disastrously and perhaps, again, aspiringly and gloriously.

5. A particular point we must pause to consider is that of sexual morality. That the irreligious mind is precluded from the apperception of the values of purity would again be a rash asseveration. Humanity in general possesses an experience of these as of other moral values—though, unenlightened by religious revelation and molding, it is mostly a stunted and rudimentary one—and sexual immorality rests, not on a literal absence of that experience but (apart from the "weakness of the flesh" proper which is apt to stifle it) on the intellectual counter-pressure of hedonistic ideologies. Now such a "repression" of the moral sense by adverse ideology is

particularly likely to occur in regard to sex morality. Moral "inhibitions" in this field, more than in any other zone of natural morality, are likely to be qualified by the humanitarian critic as superstitious, obsolete, "hostile to life," and "opposed to happiness." The reason is obvious. "Lust"—that is, inordinate sexual pleasure—typifies, in the most exemplary and characteristic manner, the concept of "sin" as such; and the valuation of purity is the very touchstone of "material" (essential, intrinsic, objective) ethics. In other words, "lust" comes nearest to the idea of a material element of life— or state of mind—"evil by itself " (the word "impure" is meant to express this) rather than evil on account of its impeding the gratification of more imperative needs or impinging upon more inviolable rights.

Perhaps it will be objected that (in Catholic ethics, for instance) the seeking of pleasure is not itself immoral, the profligate or the pervert sinning merely in that he procures himself pleasure by illicit means: just as the thief deserves reproof only because he deprives another person of his rightful property, whereas the use to which he turns the stolen object or money has (generally speaking) nothing bad in itself. However, the structure of the two situations is entirely different: in the case of theft, there is a clear disjunction between good or permissible "ends" and criminal "means," whereas in the case of "evil lust," such a separation is untenable; the circumstances which make sexual enjoyment immoral determine the quality of the pleasure in question and taint the respective experience of the subject as a whole. The situation is comparable not to the one involved in theft as it "normally" happens but to what theft would be if the thief enjoyed with intense excitement the act of stealing itself rather than the goods of which he thus unlawfully gains possession.

On the other hand, sex immorality—in its isolated typical forms, uncomplicated by violence or deceit—fails to involve any transgression of the "rights of others," or even any damage to their interests; in an immanent computation of "human needs," therefore, we may easily be driven to decide that those needs in their entirety are better served by disregarding certain "needs for chastity" than by refusing gratification to certain, more or less vehement, sensual needs proscribed by religious or traditional morality. Humanitarian ethics will, without doubt, acknowledge and stress the elementary necessity of self-control and the general readiness to exercise it; but apart from this abstract and formal postulate, definite standards of purity can hardly count on any support. The individual and social "harmfulness" of inordinate sexual pleasure *as such* being susceptible of a very vague and circuitous demonstration only, it will appear "rational" to entrust its indulgence or shunning to anybody's personal taste—and more than that, to denounce any emphatic moral standpoint and terminology in these matters as intolerant, superstitious, narrow-minded, arbitrary and obnoxious. Immoralism will sometimes make fun of our resentment at murder, robbery, cruelty, tyranny, treachery, mendacity, arrogance, etc., "unmasking" it as a manifestation of inferiority, the "instinct of revenge," "neurotic fear," or what-not; but serious and responsible humanitarianism will rarely endorse such a nihilistic attitude except in a local and accidental context. In regard to the sphere of purity, however, the outlook is darker. For here, as we have seen, adequate and objective moral experience is more intimately linked to a sense of religious mystery—a genuine belief in substantial "good" (with the concept of "holiness" hovering uncomfortably near), and in at least quasi-substantial evil. The temptation to discard this kind of moral experiences as delusive, neurotic, wayward, and requiring a thorough "rationalization" (that is, dissolution), is perilously plausible. Only think of how the vast majority of non-Catholic opinion today looks upon Catholic standards concerning contraceptives and divorce or remarriage, not as too lofty and rigorous but as frankly revolting and scandalous.

The most important consequence lies, not even so much perhaps in the actual spreading of sexual license and its biological and sociological effects, disastrous though these may be, as in the enervating and deadening action of ideological immoralism in respect of purity *upon men's moral sensibility as a whole.* The category of good and evil—of virtue and vice—being, as it were, mystically up-rooted here, a process of shrinking and flattening will blight moral life in its entirety, including even its most directly "justifiable" and "useful" manifestations. With the destruction of morality *par excellence,* the psychological center of moral fastidiousness is obliterated, the ground prepared for further corrosive "interpretations," the leverage established for the destruction of morality pure and simple.

A certain formal analogy to the theme of purity is presented by the moral problem of suicide. The *felo de se,* too, "violates nobody's rights" and merely exercises, according to his preference, his empire over himself. Here, again, the humanitarian mind is at great difficulty to find any justifiable ground for moral "interference"; and this, again, is a matter of at least great symbolic importance. Humanitarianism, while it certainly does not encourage man to practice all sorts of iniquity, portends a decisive moral *abandonment* of man.

6. Another important dimension in which the contrast between the two "attitudes" unfolds impressively is connected but by no means identical with the sphere of sexual morality. I am hinting at the rather obscure problems of generation and biological continuity; the sense of the future and the instinct of prevision; the experience of supra-individual duration. The fact that "modern" man, under the influence of what is called here irreligious humanitarianism, reveals a growing tendency to stop procreation and to view the preservation and the status of his family (as a relatively "immortal" social unit) with indifference has been much commented upon. It is not manifest that this should be so; on the contrary, it would be quite understandable that the loss of the religious belief in the soul's survival after death should strengthen the need for "surviving in one's progeny"; also humanitarianism obviously tends, not to neglect but to overemphasize the physical care for children and the task of their mental education. In fact, "enlightened" man often refrains from begetting progeny unless he feels he can guarantee the utmost degree of security regarding its physical constitution and economic position—which does not happen too frequently or abundantly. However, at the heart of this meticulous responsibleness we may again and again discover an all too anxious insistence on one's own "standard of living"—the famous "motorcar which is more indispensable than a child." Yet this is not simply a matter of greed. Rather it ensues from a pious economy, not to say a deification, of "actual human needs": that is to say, the claims of human beings existing at present (including children), or presumed as "present ones" (children whose existence is "anticipated"). The willful and "unplanned" multiplication of "claimants," with the attendant complication of "needs," is looked upon as irrational; the sovereignty of "actual needs" is incompatible with the realization of a biological or historical continuum. Hence the tendency, not only to regard contraceptive practice as laudable, but to consider even artificial abortion as more or less justifiable.

Irreligious man lives "in the moment"; his great concern about the fate of such children as he happens to have or consents to have does not mean a genuine tribute to the future but merely the incorporation of some technically "future" interests in the context of the present moment: not a genuine recognition of supra-momentary duration (which seems to presuppose a mystical experience, however vague, of eternity as mirrored in continuity throughout time) but merely a craving for "improvement," "evolution," and "expansion" essentially *immanent to the "present moment."* Whoever looks back upon the past as simply dead and done for will also lack the capacity for any organic contact with the future. And a mind must be so fashioned which rejects the idea of there being anything more holy and more objectively real than one's "actual needs" as well as those of the "other members of society" (who people one's "actual," momentary world). What is most characteristic of the full-fledged irreligious mind is not its disbelief in the immortality of the soul but its loss of the desire for immortality: the evanescence of any meaning attached thereto. This observation is not contradicted but confirmed by the "modern" tendency to ignore death, or banish it from the realm of consciousness, as though it were an unhappy accident or an indecent eccentricity, avoidable in general. Instead of the longing for a status in the order of eternity, the moment with its more and more elaborately subserved needs is set up as a substitute for eternity.

Furthermore, the severing of ties with transcendent reality also determines—subtly and slowly though this law may impose itself—a desiccation and fading away of man's psychic bonds with reality pure and simple. The "release of energies" ostensibly brought about by man's emancipation from religious concerns, anxieties and inhibitions proves temporary, illusory, and lethal. Life that has become "its own master" is bound for suicide. I will no more than mention one highly important political implication: the increasing difficulty for liberal-democratic societies of conducting a sustained foreign policy based on prevision and the sense of continuity.

7. That "culture" in the specific sense of the term—high art, and creative thought—are likely to be seared and to wither away in an age of irreligion has become almost a truism these days, although there was a time when "culture" in this high sense was expected to profit from the disappearance of religion, and also to supersede it advantageously. For it may be conceded that the initial relaxation of religion's control over men's minds may sometimes produce a stimulating and enlivening effect on thought and imagination: the first doubts concerning what was generally and unquestionably held to be true yesterday, as well as a certain measure of the freedom to disagree even in basic things, may exercise an apparently fertilizing fascination on the mind and encourage the flight of fancy. But a morbid overexcitement dissembling an inward consumptive process—a decrease of

genuine power and of recuperative faculty—will not be slow to follow, and in due course will again yield its place to manifest drabness, inertia, and mental drought. The truth is that man is as little equipped to be "imaginative" of his own force as to maintain his moral level on the resources of his own nature. Creative and constructive imagination is consistent with disbelief in the existence of its object, or with a state of evanescent religious belief in general, but it is not consistent with religious unbelief as a basic and stabilized state of mind; nor can it thrive in a social milieu sterilized of transcendent references. Imagination may not imply actual belief, but it does imply a resonance of actual belief, piety, devotion, anxiety, consciousness of one's dependence on a superior Reality: when that resonance is dead, imagination itself will crumple up and become mummified in spite of all endeavors to recapture a mystical "mood" (which is in fact only the aura attending the actual deference to a mystical reality) and of all artifices applied to "inspiring" our thoughts with the allegedly "noblest" theme of human welfare and "optimum adjustment to conditions."

Perhaps, it will be contended, the lack or ungenuineness of "high culture" can be put up with if at the same time society lives in a civilized order and a state of prosperity—including literacy and a good level of education—which is doubtless possible in logic. But is it so in reality? In this respect many doubts have been expressed. "Where there is no vision the people perish" is a slogan often to be heard today; though most of those who repeat it seem to take it for granted that the prospering of the "people" is itself the primary and proper object of the "vision." Anyhow, I may not be far wrong in assuming that a danger deeper and more dismal is inherent in spiritual inanition and levelling than the boredom and dissatisfaction of a tiny "minority" of refined intellectuals. Humanitarianism suppresses, thwarts, and stultifies too much that is by no means a mere froth upon the surface of "serious" life but belongs to the very viscera of human constitution. Whether or when the mankind of which we are will again hunger strongly and widely for the kingdom of Our Lord we do not know; but there are not a few presages that in some way or other (sociologically speaking) the "gods and demons" will, sooner and more sweepingly than many would surmise, come into their own.

More acute observers have voiced the paradoxical suspicion that the emancipation and deification of human "life's aims" may result in a decay of men's joy of life, psychic vitality, and appetite for work as well as enjoyment of pleasure. If that were true, and more than an accidental and sporadic or transitory phenomenon, it might indeed mean that humanitarianism is doomed to defeat its own ends. Some would put the blame specifically on Puritanism; but I wonder whether the old crabbed Puritans did not live with far more "gusto" and vigor than do the vitamin-conscious sovereign selves of an earth-controlling, labor-saving, "streamlined" modernity. Others would indict, precisely, mechanized production and the soulless "mass existence" it determines; but civilizations which lacked our technological temptations have revealed more or less analogous symptoms of psychic consumption after the basic faith which inspired them was gone; it seems as though our socio-economic technique of life were less a primary cause than an effect and expression of more central processes.

We will not argue at any length with the not too numerous austere moralists who allege that modern man is cloyed and oversaturated with goods and pleasures (as though the simple abundance of goods or comforts could account for the fierce obsession with prosperity; as though surfeiting itself would not indicate a wrong and one-sided kind of food, or an ill-balanced disposition on the eater's part) nor with those tenacious humanitarians who persist in denouncing "under-consumption" and this or that "maladjustment" betokening that the "economic problem" or, better still, the "cultural problem" is "not yet solved." Most of us bewail the "disproportion between mankind's stupendous progress in controlling the material forces of the world and his much less satisfactory control of moral and spiritual ones"; and this sounds fairly convincing. However, the reason does not lie in the so much greater controllability of material forces but in the fact that Man has essentially chosen to "progress" on the wrong track; and he will continue doing so as long as he dreams of "controlling moral and spiritual forces" (on the model of the material ones, of all things!) instead of surrendering to the moral and spiritual Reality outside and above him.

By formalizing, restricting, relaxing and refusing his allegiance to Him Who Is, man has set himself at war (a war waged on innumerable fronts) with Being as such, and condemned himself to seek satisfaction in the dissolution and reduction of all Substantiality and Nobility. By "emancipating" the Image from its Exemplar, the privileged Creature from its sovereign Creator, he has virtually destroyed his very humanity. He will recover his humanity (including even its undergrowth of psychic robustness) as soon as he truly and integrally reasserts the greatest and most vital of his needs, ignored and maimed and stifled by humanitarianism: the need for a meaning of his life which points decisively and majestically beyond the range of "his needs."

Selected Bibliography

Aristotle. *The Politics*. Translated by Carnes Lord. Chicago: University of Chicago Press, 2013.

Aron, Raymond. *Main Currents of Sociological Thought*, Vol. 1. New Brunswick, NJ: Transaction Publishers, 1998.

Benedict XVI (Pope Emeritus). "Instruction on Liberation Theology." In *The Essential Pope Benedict: His Central Speeches and Writings*, edited by John F. Thornton and Susan B. Varenne. New York: HarperCollins, 2007.

———. *Jesus of Nazareth*. Translated by Adrian J. Walker. New York: Doubleday, 2007.

———. "Regensburg Address." In *Liberating Logos: Pope Benedict's September Speeches*, edited by Marc D. Guerra. South Bend, IN: St. Augustine's Press, 2014.

———. "Conscience and Truth." In *Values in a Time of Upheaval*. New York: Crossroad Publishing, 2006.

Besançon, Alain. *The Falsification of the Good: Soloviev and Orwell*. Translated by Matthew Screech. London: Claridge Press, 1994.

Brownson, Orestes. *The Convert: Or, Leaves from My Experience*. Edited by Arnie J. Griffioen. Milwaukee, WI: Marquette University Press, 2012.

Comte, August. *System of Positive Polity*, Vol. 1. Translated by John Henry Bridges. New York: Burt Franklin, 1875.

Francis (Pope). *The Joy of the Gospel: Evangelii Gaudium*. New York: Image Books, 2013.

———. *The Name of God Is Mercy: A Conversation with Andrea Tornielli*. New York: Random House, 2016

———. *Pope Francis Speaks to the United States and Cuba: Speeches, Homilies, and Interviews.* Huntington, IN: Our Sunday Visitor Press, 2015.

———. *Praise Be to You (Laudato Si'): On Care for Our Common Home.* San Francisco: Ignatius Press, 2015.

———. *Recontres avec Dominique Wolton: Politique et Société.* Paris: Éditions de l'Observatoire, 2017.

Gress, Carrie. "What Exactly is Social Justice?" *National Catholic Register*, March 3, 2016.

Habermas, Jürgen. *The Lure of Technology.* Translated by Ciaran Cronin. New York: Polity Press, 2015.

Jouvenel, Bertrand de. *Sovereignty: An Inquiry into the Political Good.* Translated by J. F. Huntington. Indianapolis, IN: Liberty Fund, 1997.

Kolnai, Aurel. *Politics, Values, and National Socialism.* Edited by Graham McAleer. New Brunswick, NJ: Transaction Publishers, 2013.

———. *Privilege and Liberty and Other Essays in Political Philosophy.* Edited by Daniel J. Mahoney. Lexington Books, 1999.

———. *The Utopian Mind and Other Papers.* Edited by Francis Dunlop. London: Athlone, 1995.

Krasnov, Vladislav. "Wrestling with Lev Tolstoi: War, Peace and Revolution in Aleksandr Solzhenitsyn's New *Avgust Chetyrnadstatogo.*" *Slavic Review* 45, No. 4 (Winter 1986): 707–719.

Lawler, Peter. "Introduction." In Orestes Brownson, *The American Republic.* Wilmington, DE: ISI Books, 2003.

Lubac, Henri de. *The Drama of Atheistic Humanism.* Translated by Mark Sebanc. San Francisco: Ignatius Press, 1995.

Manent, Pierre. *Beyond Radical Secularism: How France and the Christian West Should Respond to the Islamic Challenge.* Translated by Ralph C. Hancock. South Bend, IN: St. Augustine's Press, 2016.

———. "Human Unity Real and Imagined." *First Things*, October 2012.

———. *Seeing Things Politically: Interviews with Bénédicte Delorme-Montini.* Translated by Ralph C. Hancock. South Bend, IN: St. Augustine's Press, 2015.

———. "La tentation de l'humanitaire." *Géopolitique*, no. 68 (2000).

———. *A World beyond Politics? A Defense of the Nation-State.* Translated by Marc Le Pain. Princeton, NJ and Oxford: Princeton University Press, 2006.

McAleer, G. J. *To Kill Another: Homicide and Natural Law.* New Brunswick, NJ: Transaction Publishers, 2012.

Nivat, Georges. *Le phénomène Soljénitsyne.* Paris: Fayard, 2009.

Péguy, Charles. *Temporal and Eternal.* Translated by Alexander Dru. Indianapolis, IN: Liberty Fund, 2001.

Reinsch, Richard M., II, ed. *Seeking the Truth: An Orestes Brownson Anthology.* Washington, DC: Catholic University of America Press, 2016.

Sarah, Robert (Cardinal). *God or Nothing: A Conversation on Faith with Nicolas Diat.* San Francisco: Ignatius Press, 2015.

Schall, James V. (S. J.) "Concerning the 'Ecological' Path to Salvation." *Catholic World Report,* June 21, 2015.

———. *The Regensburg Lecture.* South Bend, IN: St. Augustine's Press, 2007.

Soloviev, Vladimir. *Politics, Law, and Morality: Essays by V. S. Soloviev.* Edited and translated by Vladimir Wozniuk. New Haven, CT: Yale University Press, 2000.

———. *Sophia, God & A Short Tale of the Antichrist: Also Including At the Dawn of Mist-Shrouded Youth.* Translated by Boris Jakim. Semantron Press, 2014.

———. *War, Progress, and the End of History: Three Conversations.* Translated by Alexander Bakshy. Revised by Thomas R. Beyer, Jr. Lindisfarne Press, 1990.

Solzhenitsyn, Aleksandr. *August 1914.* Translated by H. T. Willetts. New York: Farrar, Straus and Giroux, 1989.

———. *March 1917.* Book 1. Translated by Marian Schwartz. Notre Dame, IN: University of Notre Dame Press, 2017.

———. *November 1916.* Translated by H. T. Willets. New York: Farrar, Straus and Giroux, 1999.

———. *The Solzhenitsyn Reader: New and Essential Writings, 1947–2005.* Edited by Edward E. Ericson, Jr., and Daniel J. Mahoney. Wilmington, DE: ISI Books, 2006.

Tocqueville, Alexis de. *Democracy in America.* Translated by Arthur Goldhammer. New York: Library of America, 2004.

Tolstoy, Leo. *The Life of Jesus: The Gospel in Brief.* Translated by Dustin Condren. New York: Harper Perennial, 2011.

———. *War and Peace.* Translated by Richard Pevear and Larissa Volokhonsky. New York: Vintage Classics, 2008.

Voegelin, Eric. *From Enlightenment to Revolution.* Edited by John H. Hallowell. Durham, NC: Duke University Press, 1975.

Will, George F. "Pope Francis's fact-free flamboyance." *Washington Post,* September 18, 2015.

Index